THE
ULTIMATE WEALTH

CHEN GONG WAH

Copyright © 2019 by Ocean Productions
All rights reserved. No part of this book may be reproduced, scanned, or distributed in any printed or electronic form without permission.
New Edition: October 2019
Printed in the United States of America
ISBN: 1645505332
ISBN: 9781645505334

TABLE OF CONTENTS

Author's Notes vii
Acknowledgments ix

1. The Old Man Called In The Debt 1
2. The Old Man Talked To His Grandson 6
3. The Student Met The Master 9
4. The Lessons Began 13
5. The Student Learnt Of His Identity And Relationship With The Universe 18
6. The Student Learnt To Be Powerful 24
7. The Student Learnt To Place An Order With The Universe 30
8. The Student Learnt To Create Through Visualisation And Prayer 37
9. The Student Learnt To Co-Create With The Universe 41
10. The Student Successfully Practised Co-Creation 47
11. The Student Learnt To Manage A Difficult Personality 52
12. The Student Learnt About Dis-Eases And How To Heal 56
13. The Student Learnt The Keys To Health, Happiness And Abundance 63
14. Reunion 71
15. The Student Learnt About The Personal Universe 79
16. The Student Learnt To Access His Own Personal Universe 85
17. The Student Unearthed His Personal Treasures 94
18. The Teacher Met With Resistance 106
19. The Student Learnt About Aspects And Mirrors 113
20. The Student Released His Defences Around His Stories 119

21. The Student Learnt The Importance Of Creating A Safe Haven.. 129
22. The Student Played The Teacher 136
23. The Students Began Conscious Breathing 145
24. The Student Learnt To Release His Vows Of Poverty And Resistance To Wealth... 152
25. The Student Learnt The Importance Of Praise And Gratitude 158
26. The Student Graduated... 165

AUTHOR'S NOTES

This book is written for all who seek to know more about themselves so that in the reading and the soul searching, some inner truth may be triggered to reveal the glory of the Divine Self within.

For easy understanding, I have written it in fiction form and organised it into two sections – Book One and Book Two. The story is about a fifteen year old boy who came under the tutelage of an enlightened Qi Gong master who taught him the Secrets of the Universe. As the story unfolds, the boy discovered his real identity and how, by using certain techniques and practices, he could come into his own power, the power of love, the power of Being, from which he could manifest anything he wanted.

The plot, characters and references to places in this story are purely imaginary. But the explanations and techniques mentioned are valid and workable, based on my knowledge and experience. However, I hold no responsibility for choices made and techniques used by readers because of differences between individuals, their perceptions, interpretations, assessments and circumstances.

This book seeks only to entertain and open up minds to the magnificence of our Godself which is our true source of love, happiness and well-being.

All My Love, Happy Reading!

ACKNOWLEDGMENTS

A great part of what I know and what I've written is largely influenced by the teachings of ascended masters and enlightened beings – Lord Sananda (Jesus Christ) through Sal Rachele; Emmanuel through Pat Rodegast; Bartholomew through Mary- Margaret Moore and Light Beings –Kryon through Lee Carroll; Orin and Daben through Sanaya Roman and Duanne Packer, the Pleiadians through AmorahQuan Yin and Heyoan through Barbara Brennan. My knowledge of chakra healing comes from the late Master Dr Luong Minh Dang and Dr Edgoh Bee and friends while my co-creation capabilities are honed based on the teachings of Masami Saionji, Tobias, Adamus St Germain and a number of other angels of whom I do not even know the name as they came to me and got my agreement to download the information to me as I slept.

To all who have helped to bring me to who I am today, I am immensely grateful – thank you.

I would like to specially highlight the support, guidance and encouragement of Father God without Whom this book would not have been written and I would like to say that we have an extraordinary relationship that is precious beyond words. Thank you, Father. I love you.

My gratitude also goes to my family for their continual love and support, particularly during the writing of this book which span more than ten years because I needed to get to the bottom of *why things happened the way they did* – I am still learning…and life is still unfolding… oh, yes. So, thank you. I love you all.

ONE

THE OLD MAN CALLED IN THE DEBT

Penang, 1999

The old man trudged up the hill with a walking stick in one hand and a bag of fruits in the other. Every now and then, he would stop to rest his walking stick against a tree or rock and wipe off the perspiration from his face and neck. Although the weather had been fine when he started out from his home that morning, the sun had soon moved overhead. The sprinkling of clouds in the sky was not sufficient cover and there were few breezes to cool his body which was getting warmer with each step. It was an arduous climb but one that could not be held off any longer.

His grandson, Hai San, had turned fifteen just two months ago and was fast growing up into a young man. Having lost both his parents and a younger sister through a freak accident when he was ten, he had been brought up by the old man. Intelligent, sensitive and cheeky at times, he had rapidly become the old man's favourite amongst the latter's dozen odd grandchildren. With a tragedy behind him and without the love and support of a complete family environment, the old man had feared that the boy would grow up, lacking the confidence of boys his own age. Fortunately, the reverse was true. Even so, the old man could not help being concerned about the boy's future. Who would care for his grandson whom he loved more than life itself after he was gone? Who would be there for him? He could not expect his daughters to do it for they had their own families to think of. Oh, he had no doubt they could provide Hai San with food and shelter but he was thinking more in terms of the intangible quality of life such as love, happiness, moral support, confidence and trust which were difficult enough for some people to comprehend, much less to provide. Neither could he expect the boy's maternal relatives to step in as guardians as they themselves lived troubled lives. No, his grandson deserved better and he would ensure that the boy receive special training to enable him to live a fulfilling life even if his methods were, albeit, unconventional.

Old Man Huang had heard through the coffee-shop grapevine in Air Itam that Sifu Wang had encountered a transformational experience some twenty years ago and held certain divine secrets of the universe. Sifu Wang had become a legend overnight and had attracted students by the hundreds each month for qi gong and martial arts lessons. Of the Secrets, however, it remained a mystery as to how many had the opportunity to receive the training. Nevertheless, Sifu Wang's fame had spread far and wide, eventually reaching the shores of Singapore, Thailand, Indonesia and even Australia.

Both Old Man Huang and Sifu Wang had originated from the same village in China and their families had been friendly with each other. But both had gone separate ways and lived different lives since coming to then Malaya. In the heart of each one, though, the memory of a secret debt was kept; the former's father had helped the latter's family escaped to safety during the Anti Movements Campaign in the early 1950s.

Sifu Wang's residence was located near the Air Itam Reservoir. Every morning, retirees and health enthusiasts would hike up the three to four kilometers of narrow road to perform their daily exercises. But as soon as the sun was up, the road would become deserted except for some motorcyclists and the odd Public Works vehicles that served the area. But that very morning, the old man was undeterred. What were a few kilometers and a bit of sun anyway? What was more important was to get his mission accomplished.

• • •

"It's been a long time," said Sifu Wang in Chinese, over a cup of tea. "How have you been, my Brother?"

"As good as can be, at my age. I can't complain," replied the old man who, at sixty-eight, was eight years older than the former.

"And your family?"

"They are well, thank you for your concern," replied the old man.

Sifu Wang smilingly nodded in acknowledgement.

"And how about you, Sifu?" Old Man Huang asked. "How have you been?"

"Great, great," Sifu Wang replied.

"And your family?"

"They are very well, thank you for asking after them. Are you still in the bicycle repair business, Brother?' asked Sifu Wang.

"Yes, I still dabbled in it to pass the time. But the bulk of the business is long gone as young people nowadays prefer to ride motor cycles," the old man returned. "Er...I've heard that Sifu Wang is a legend and your students number by the thousands."

"Not anymore. In the old days, perhaps," Sifu Wang laughingly accepted the compliment. "I'm now retired," Sifu Wang revealed. "These days, I am more often than not, either pottering in my garden or learning new things. I've even started learning how to use a computer and as they say, 'surf the net'."

He turned and proudly pointed to his brand new desktop at the corner. "Look! That's a gift from my grandchildren. They've as good as told me that I'm behind the times – outdated! Hence, this gadget," Sifu Wang chuckled, recalling the memory.

"These young people!" Old Man Huang joined in, shaking his head.

There was a comfortable silence while both men sipped their tea, each remembering their days of youth and marveling at how fast time had flown by. Forty years was suddenly condensed into a few minutes as memories flashed past in quick succession. Outside, the magpies were chirping and the faint humming sounds of jungle insects could be heard.

Finally, Old Man Huang broke the silence. "Sifu, you must know that I've come here today for a purpose?"

"Absolutely," Sifu Wang replied. "How may I be of help to you, Brother?"

"I seek your compassion on an old friend, Sifu. It's my grandson – Hai San who needs help and he is the only grandson I have who carries my family name. I've looked after him ever since my son and daughter-in-law passed away in an accident. But I am getting old and in no way proficient in teaching a fifteen year old boy the ways of the world. I seek your kindness to extend a helping hand and take him under your wing and train him. In that way, my heart will be at peace knowing that he can fend for himself when I am no longer around," Old Man Huang appealed.

Sifu Wang nodded understandingly while he gave the matter some thought. "Even though I have retired, Brother, it will be ungrateful of me to turn down your request," he conceded. "What type of training do you have in mind?"

Old Man Huang leaned forward eagerly and answered in a hush tone, "I am thinking of *the Secrets*."

Sifu Wang jerked with surprise. It had been almost a decade since he last trained a disciple on the Secrets. The Secrets were reputed to restore Divine Life and Divine Riches to humans. To receive them, one had to train in the moral teaching for years and even then, not anybody would be eligible. Only an enlightened Master of The Secrets could decide on who was fit to receive the training. *How then could a fifteen year old boy be entrusted with such a profound and esoteric teaching?*

Sifu Wang stood up and walked to the window. He was silent while he steadily gazed out. In the room the sound of a clock ticking away could be heard.

Old Man Huang shifted uncomfortably in his chair. He cringed at his own audacity. He had gambled away his only ace and it now looked like it was not going to bear any positive result. Possibly, he would lose a friend as well for Sifu Wang had been kind and hospitable. And his grandson would not have any training to turn him from a common Joe into a person of substance.

Finally, Sifu Wang turned back from the window and said gravely, "You ask for the impossible, Brother. The Secrets is not just any training. It's a training that is given only to those who are ready."

"Surely an exception can be made?"

"Exceptions have never been made, Brother."

"Sifu, pardon me for saying this. But do you think giving back one life is too much to ask for the six lives which were saved?

Sifu Wang regarded the old man steadily. "You drive a hard bargain, Brother. Those who are given the training know how to care for it and not to misuse it."

"My grandson is a responsible young man."

"At fifteen, he is a juvenile."

"I can vouch for his maturity and integrity."

"You are serious, aren't you?"

"I'm never been more serious in my life, Sifu."

"What if I can't take him on?"

"I hate to see a debt unpaid."

Sifu Wang smiled. The old man knew where to put his punches, alright. "I'll let you know in a few days, Brother, after I have meditated on it. But I make no promises. Do you have a picture of your grandson, by any chance?"

The old man nodded. Eagerly and with trembling hands, he opened his wallet, extracted a stamp-sized photograph and handed it to Sifu Wang.

Sifu Wang gazed at it quietly and smiled. Then he patted the old man's shoulder in a friendly gesture. "I'll call you when I've decided, Brother."

TWO

THE OLD MAN TALKED TO HIS GRANDSON

Three days later...

Old Man Huang selected a choice piece of Curry Chicken drumstick and placed it on his grandson's plate of rice. "Eat up. There's peanut soup for you afterwards."

Hai San eagerly dug his fork into the chicken meat and pierced it apart with his spoon before dipping a morsel into his mouth. With his mouth half full, he enquired, "Why do I always have to drink peanut soup, Grandpa?"

"Because it'll make you into a strong man."

"Oh yea? I don't recall any of my friends in school having to drink it," he mumbled.

"Do you hate it that much?"

"No, really, Grandpa. It's just boring, that's all," the boy replied and continued munching his food.

"Well, sometimes the most boring thing in the world can turn out to be the most rewarding except we don't know it until years later," the old man admonished.

"Like what?"

"Like a good education, Boy. There's no substitute for a good education," the old man continued, observing the boy. "Have you finished or do you want more rice?"

"Want more rice. I'll get it myself, Grandpa. Can I get some for you, too?"

"No, thanks, I've finished."

The old man waited until his grandson had finished his dinner before he started talking again.

"Hai San, have you ever thought about what you're going to do after you finish school?"

"Yes, Grandpa, I want to be an E&E engineer."

"How're you going to finance it?"

"Study hard, get a scholarship."

"Good, good, what if you can't get a scholarship?"

"Then I'll get a job first and save up to do off-campus."

The old man studied his grandson's determined face. He was not surprised. He had known ever since the boy came to live with him that the latter had a mind of his own and was not averse to hard work. However, his proposed methods to achieve his ambition, albeit honest, could hardly have won any prize for creativity. Almost everybody the same age was thinking along the same direction. How could a person succeed with so much competition? Why should he have to compete, anyway? It's stupid and tedious to always follow the herd, the old man thought. It was fortunate that Sifu Wang had agreed to his request.

"What if I tell you that there is an easier way and you can achieve your ambition faster than you think?"

"Rob the bank, you mean?" the boy grinned at his grandfather, over the peanut soup.

"That would be the fastest way to jail!" retorted the old man. "No, I mean get a kind of training that would make you, say, smarter than other people and able to solve any problem that you encounter, financial or otherwise."

The boy paused in the midst of drinking his soup. *What was his grandfather talking about? Had he gone nuts or something?*

"I want you to be well equipped when you go out into the world, Boy," the old man continued. "And that means not just having a fancy certificate and sitting in an air-cond place, with the computers and all. Those are just superficial trappings. Come war, earthquake, economic depression and what have you, all these will be useless! Useless-you understand?"

The boy nodded. That, at least, made sense.

"I want you to get the type of training that will stand good in any situation. Come rain or shine, good days or bad days, you will still do well," the old man asserted.

"Well, what do you have in mind, Grandpa? It sounds – omnipotent!" Hai San jested.

"I am not joking, Boy!" The old man looked at his grandson sternly. Then he continued, "The school holidays will be here in just two weeks. It will be as good an opportunity for you to start training in something really useful. My good old friend from China, Sifu Wang has agreed to take you on as his student."

"To train in what, Grandpa?"

"*The Secrets of the Universe.*"

"The what!" Hai San nearly choked on the last drop of peanut soup.

"*The Secrets of the Universe.* Now, don't take this lightly." The old man looked at his grandson sternly. "Sifu Wang is an extraordinary teacher like no other," he continued. "To be his student is a privilege money cannot buy. Remember that, my Boy."

Hai San's shoulders started to shake with laughter. The temptation to tell his grandfather that it was all '*bull shit*' and that he had been had died in his throat at the look on his grandfather's face. He sobered himself quickly.

Are there really such things as the Secrets? He wondered. *Or has his Grandpa been duped by this so-called friend?*

"What's up, Boy?"

"Er...nothing. Just that...how much money did you have to pay this Master, Grandpa?" he asked.

"Nothing! That's the best part. He was returning me a favour. Call it paying off an old debt if you like." The old man smiled in satisfaction.

"So, when do I start training?"

"I thought we could go over to Sifu Wang's place on Friday, the eleventh to get you introduced. Then, you can start on Monday, the fourteenth. Is that okay with you?"

"Yes," Hai San replied, poker-faced.

THREE

THE STUDENT MET THE MASTER

Two weeks later...

"Don't forget, Hai San. We are meeting Sifu Wang at 9.30 tomorrow morning. You should sleep earlier tonight," Old Man Huang reminded his grandson from the doorway, amidst the cacophony of the computer game.

"Ok, Grandpa-I'm finishing my game now," Hai San replied, still staring keenly at the monitor.

As soon as his grandfather had closed the door, Hai San gave a sigh. *Why do I have to meet this man?* As if in answer, his grandfather's words echoed back in his head like a tape recorder:

'.........*Sifu Wang has agreed to train you in the secrets of the universe..... you can achieve your ambition faster than you think... Sifu Wang is an extraordinary teacher like no other..... To be his student is a privilege money cannot buy.*'

It was totally preposterous, of course. Hai San did not believe that it would be possible for anybody to know the secrets of the universe, let alone master them to make things happen. Why, it would be-magic! Yet, he couldn't help being drawn to the possibility. He had been privately excited at the idea and had felt his heart beat faster at his grandfather's announcement, despite his outward nonchalant attitude.

If it were really true...and this man was as good as what his grandfather had said, he would be very powerful. Why, he would be the most powerful man on earth! *If I learn under him, I will be powerful, too – in time – and I will not need to fear anything anymore – no fear of failure, no fear of bullies, no fear of poverty, no fear of illness.... I could be anything I want. I would be – invincible!*

His reverie was interrupted by a couple of knocks on the door which were a reminder by his grandfather to close up for the night.

"Ok, Grandpa, I'm done," Hai San yelled in reply.

Minutes later, he shut down his computer and went to brush his teeth. As he got ready for bed, his mind started to wonder about the next day's meeting. Friday the eleventh! *Would it be a turning point in his life? Or just a day to be wasted? Would Sifu Wang be a tough taskmaster like those he had read about in books or a kind old soul like his grandfather? Or was he a lousy trickster on ego trips, giving an old man false hopes with exaggerated claims of divine powers?* He lay in the semi-darkness, trying to figure out the likes of a man whom he had only recently known by name. He gave a big yawn. Well, he would just have to be patient. It was only another eleven hours away...

• • •

Sifu Wang was unlike anybody the boy had met. For one thing, he did not put on any of the airs of a so-called successful person. Instead, he was simple and straightforward, not unlike his grandfather. But there were clear differences between them, apart from their age. Sifu Wang looked happy and relaxed and like a man who was in full control of himself. He exuded an aura that the boy found indescribable. It was as if his very presence brightened up the room and the boy couldn't help recalling his heart flutter for a few moments during the introductions. Sifu's eyes were also clear and penetrating as if they could see straight into your soul. But they were eyes that smiled.

After coffee was served, Sifu Wang surprised the boy by asking directly, "Hai San, tell me why you are interested to learn such a vast and profound subject as *The Secrets*."

Unprepared, Hai San began to search in his mind for an answer. "I'm afraid I don't know anything about this subject, Sifu," he managed to get out apologetically. "But having met you, I have this yearning in my heart to know what you know."

"Why?"

"Because …because then I can become a super person like you," Hai San replied.

Sifu Wang laughed aloud. "*The Secrets* is the intimate Knowledge and Mastery of Self and the Universe," he explained. "It is the Way, the Connection to one's own Divinity, one's own Godself. When one finds It, the entire universe is at one's disposal. True happiness, abundance, love, you name it – all of them are available at the mere wish of one's heart. But this Secret of Secrets had been hidden from men for so long that men had forgotten about it. Whoever knows It holds a responsibility, a very high responsibility indeed, to use It properly."

Sifu Wang regarded the boy solemnly and continued. "At this moment, the Secrets is held only in the hands of a few thousands on planet Earth. Because there are still people who are unscrupulous enough to abuse it for their own personal selfish aims, the Secrets can be taught only to those who are genuinely operating for Good."

Then he stressed, "I will teach you on *two* conditions, provided you are really interested,"

"Oh, I am! I'm really interested!" the boy exclaimed, excitedly. Then he leaned forward and asked, "Tell me the conditions, Sifu."

"Relax, Boy, relax," his grandfather advised gently.

"Firstly, that whatever I teach you, you should keep secret. That means, no boasting around or telling other people that you can do such and such a thing. Secondly, you can only use it for a good purpose to benefit yourself and others and never for harm. Have I made myself clear?"

"Yes, Sifu!" the boy replied. He couldn't stop a smile from breaking over his face. "Shall we shake hands on it?"

Sifu Wang smiled broadly before extending his hand. They shook hands vigorously with the old man as witness.

"When can he start his training, Sifu?" the old man asked.

"About a week from now, say Monday, the 21st of November, if Hai San is free."

"I am," the boy replied promptly, mentally reminding himself to cancel any other engagements. "How long will this training take, Sifu?"

"God knows. Two years, five years, maybe a lifetime. It depends on how fast you master the Secrets."

With that, Hai San rolled his eyes and breathed in deeply. "I'll persevere. Don't worry, Sifu. I'll be a good student."

Sifu Wang looked amused. "You don't know yet until you are put to the test."

"I can't thank you enough, Sifu," the old man said.

"It's my pleasure, Brother," Sifu Wang replied.

FOUR

THE LESSONS BEGAN

"Do you know," Sifu Wang asked, "the difference between a really powerful person and a not so powerful person?"

At this question, Hai San sat up and thought for a while and said, "I think it's a matter of degrees of energy."

"Not quite. Try again."

"How about the ability to impact change on others?"

"Hmm. What you are telling me are actually attributes of power. I'll tell you the difference. A really powerful person knows who he is whereas a not so powerful person thinks he knows but he doesn't."

Hai San was perplexed. "So, what does that mean and what does that have to do with *me*?"

"You want to be your own person, don't you? You want to be happy, successful and able to make favourable things happen, don't you? That's why you are here. So to be all that, you must wake up to who you are. Until you wake up to who you really are, you will always be working within limitations, forever being unhappy and not achieving your optimum potential. In that state, you are vulnerable to fear and negative controls by external factors. This is the prevailing situation with most people today. To transcend this state, you need to operate from your own power centre. That can come only from realization of who you are. Now, I want you to take a piece of paper and write down everything that you think you are, every description you can think of. I give you fifteen minutes to do this exercise."

Sifu Wang then walked out of the room.

Hai San scratched his head. What a strange assignment, as if he didn't know who he was!

He took a pen and ruler and started to draw a vertical line right across the middle of the page. On one half of it, he wrote down numbers one to ten and on the other, he continued the numbering to twenty. Then he started to write down his identity:

1. Huang Hai San
2. Son of the late Mr Huang Ming Hin and Madam Tan Siew Geok
3. Brother to late Ms Huang Hui Lee
4. Grandson of Mr Huang Mu
5. Grandson to the bicycle repair operator
6. Fifteen years old
7. Born in 1984
8. Stands five feet, eight inches tall
9. Weighs 65 Kg
10. Form Three Student
11. Student of SMS Methodist
12. School badminton player
13. Committee member in Literary and Debating Society
14. Quite intelligent (!)
15. Decent looking (!)
16. Ambitious
17. Friendly
18. Kind to animals
19. Basically honest
20. Loves computer games

Having filled up the page, the boy got up and wandered around the room, looking at the various knick-knacks belonging to Sifu Wang. He picked up a hollow round structure with flower motives, the size of a football, and peered from one end to another.

"That's a Merkaba," Sifu Wang said, almost startling the boy who had not heard him entering the room.

"What's it for?"

"It's a representation of the flower of life. We have this energy pattern all over us."

"Really?" the boy asked curiously.

"Really. But, that's a huge subject in itself. For now, we will focus on the basic and most important topic."

"Which is Me!"

"Yes, that's right – You! Tell me what you are."

So the boy read out aloud the entire list, his face turning redder and redder with embarrassment. Upon finishing, he stole a look at Sifu Wang to gauge the latter's reaction.

"Not bad. But all these attributes which you deemed your identity belong to what we call the 'personality'. The personality is the outward show of a person. It is only the costume. It is not the real identity."

"Then what is my real identity? Is it the mind?"

"No, it is not the mind. The mind is the thinking apparatus. It is the tool with which you currently use to help you run your life."

"So, what am I? Who am I? How is it that I don't even know myself?" Hai San cried out frustratedly.

Sifu Wang laughed. "Sit down and I'll tell you."

Hai San flopped down onto the nearest sofa and looked at Sifu Wang with anticipation. For some unknown reason, his heart began to thump quite loudly and he wondered if Sifu Wang was aware. Quite likely, he thought, otherwise why would Sifu Wang be regarding him quizzically?

"Hai San, before I begin, I want you to make a commitment to yourself. The information that I am going to impart to you in the next few minutes is *the Secret* of secrets. But, because we have all been taught differently, you may not accept it immediately. That is fine. However, there will come a time when you will have to accept it. Your own heart will increasingly tell you that."

Hai San placed a hand onto his heart. *Oh my God, Sifu knows,* he thought.

"What commitment, Sifu?"

"That irrespective of whether you believe or not what I'm going to tell you, you will keep an open mind, at least for the next six months."

"Ok."

"Are you sure?"

"Very sure."

"Right. Some of the things that I am going to tell you are of things beyond the third dimension which is the way, the limited way, we perceive our world. To understand, you have to expand your mind and use a bit of imagination. Can you do that?"

"Yes, Sifu."

"Good. As I've said, we are not who we think we are. We are, in reality, God or if you like, angels, in human form. The divine and human parts of us are inexorably intertwined, like breathing in and breathing out. The moment we choose Love, we tune into our divinity-we connect with the energy of the God Most High. In that instance, we stand at the vast expanse of infinity and are free to manifest our Magnificence, our Abundance, our Joy. In that state, no problem remains a problem. Every challenge gets resolved with its appropriate solution. However, the moment we forgo Love, we slip back into our humanness-we are back again into limitations, into challenges, into worries and all the pettiness that humans involve themselves in. You got that so far?"

Hai San frowned. "I... think so."

"Imagine life as a continuous pulsation. With each beat of the heart and each breath, you move from remembering your divinity into forgetfulness and back into remembering again. Thus, the trick to being a really powerful person is to sustain the moments of Love. The more we choose Love, the more connected we are to our divinity. And therefore, the happier and the more creative we are and the more abundant we feel. Conversely, the more we deny Love, the more egoistic we become and the more negative things we think up. This denial is Fear. Hate, anger, jealousy, meanness and greed are all aspects of Fear. They are the creations of the ego. The more we relate to the ego, the more we confine ourselves to the limitations of illusion."

Sifu Wang stopped for a moment and looked curiously at Hai San. "Are we asleep or confused now?"

Hai San blinked and grinned bashfully. "Neither." Then he asked, "Sifu, why are we part angel and part human. Why can't we be fully angel or fully human?"

"Well, we can be all of those. But it requires an extraordinary ability to change our vibrations at will."

"Sifu, how did angels and human beings come about?"

"It's a long story, Hai San. It goes back to creation and the various events in the universe."

"Tell me, Sifu, tell me, please? I love stories," Hai San pleaded.

Sifu Wang picked up his cup of coffee and took a few sips before he answered. "We will go through that in your next lesson."

But Hai San wanted to unravel into the mystery further. And he wanted it like now. He looked appealingly and expectantly at Sifu Wang.

Sifu Wang looked at the boy and laughed, shaking his head. "Drink your orange juice, Hai San. You've learnt enough for today. We'll continue next week."

With that, Hai San emptied his glass and had to be satisfied.

FIVE

THE STUDENT LEARNT OF HIS IDENTITY AND RELATIONSHIP WITH THE UNIVERSE

"Tell me what you learned in our last lesson."

Sifu Wang had walked into the room and raised enquiring eyes at the boy who hastily took off his ear phones and switched off the music on the stereo.

"Well, umm…" Hai San began, clearing his throat and trying to recall. "I learnt that I am ….part God, …part human and that I can alternate between being God and being Human through my breaths. When we connect with Love, we remember and express the divinity in us and we can manifest happiness, abundance and solutions to our problems. But when we alienate ourselves from Love, we succumb to the limitations of being human," Hai San said, looking at Sifu Wang uncertainly.

"Good. Today, we will learn about what it means to be god and how we are all related in this Universe. Are you mentally ready?" Sifu Wang asked. "Or are you still with Faye Wong (Chinese singer)?"

"I'm ready," Hai San grinned.

"Good. Remember what I said about opening your mind and expanding your imagination? You'll need a lot of that today." Sifu Wang began.

Hai San nodded and waited for Sifu Wang to continue.

"Now we'll start our lesson with a bit of practical exercise. I want you to relax, close your eyes and take three deep breaths." Sifu Wang paused to make sure that the boy was following him. Then he continued, "Imagine – imagine that everywhere around you there is nothingness except light, an expanse of intense pure white light. Imagine the beauty of this pure white light. It glows brilliantly with love and intelligence… have you imagined it?"

"Yes," Hai San whispered, eyes closed.

"Now the white light is expanding and embracing you…it is seeping into your body, filling up your body cells. Your body is now pure white light. In fact, you can't differentiate yourself from the white light. You are it and it is you. Stay with this white light for twenty minutes. Imagine it getting brighter and brighter with each second. I'll tell you when it's time to open your eyes."

So the boy did as he was told. He imagined the light. He was in it and the light was in him and it was turning brighter and brighter. Soon it began to expand. It expanded to cover his home, his district, his country and soon the whole planet. It moved into the universe, covering the planets, the stars and the sun. The universe merged with another universe and another universe. The light was getting stronger, more intense now …

Bang! The door slammed and the boy awoke with a start. His universe of light had exploded and fragmented into a billion sparks.

"What happened, Sifu?"

Sifu Wang smiled. "I should be asking you this question, Hai San. What happened to your light?"

"It exploded into a billion sparks."

"Excellent! And how do you feel?"

"Startled-kind of frightened." Hai San could still feel his heart pumping madly.

Sifu Wang nodded. "What you've just experienced is a mere illustration of how the world was formed."

"The world was formed-in this way?" Hai San widened his eyes with disbelief.

"Simplistically speaking. At the beginning there was God – The Source of All That Is. God was and is Everything that Love is. It knew Itself as Love but could not experience Itself. So It decided to create a world separate from Itself, a world of illusion, a world which was the opposite of what it was so that It could experience Itself. This differentiation began with a number of 'Big Bangs' – you must have heard of the Big Bang that scientists had been speculating for ages? Well, there was not just one Big Bang but multiple bangs. As a result several billions of fragments of God energy exploded into multi-universes and flooded into space."

Sifu Wang looked at Hai San and smiled. "The fragments of God energy or units of light consciousness which we now call 'souls' are creative and have every attribute of God within them. These original fragments further split up into smaller and smaller fragments. We – are all offsprings of the billions of fragmented energy. In other words, we are all individuations of God."

Hai San's eyes shone. It was incredulous. He had never thought of himself as holy or in any way related to the divine.

"This God energy is in everything," Sifu Wang continued. "At the lowest level are the pure elements, next come the minerals, the plants, the animals and humans. At the very beginning when humans were first created, they were capable of experiencing seven different dimensions simultaneously. The human body could change its vibrations at will; one nano-second it could be an angel flying through space and another it could be a human being walking or dancing. However, the angelic part of us was eventually forgotten. Planet earth was not only a desirable place of habitation, it was also designed to function as an inter-galactic centre. As a result, many wars between star beings were fought off the Earth for control of the planet. Have you watched the movies – the Star Wars?"

"Oh, yes, Sifu!" Hai San replied excitedly.

"It was something like that," Sifu Wang said. "Suffice to say, the conquerors raped and killed the conquered. Humans were not spared. The suffering, the aggression and the fears that were perpetuated eventually caused the human bodies to become denser and denser and over time, the memories of angelhood faded away."

Sifu Wang picked up his glass of fruit punch and took a few sips. Hai San followed suit.

"So, everything in this world is God's creation, Hai San – you, I, the trees, the animals, the mountains, the rivers as well as the illusion of fear, pain, disease and suffering," Sifu Wang concluded. "Since God has gifted us with Himself and the opportunity of *free choice,* it's all up to us whether we want to vibrate ourselves back to our inherent godly nature or remain stuck in the created illusion. Which would you choose, Hai San?"

"Can we have both, Sifu?"

"Be a God in this world, you mean?"

"Yes, I would choose to exercise godly qualities and still remain in this world."

Sifu Wang let out a guffaw. "Spoken like a true angelic warrior! What do you understand by being godly?"

"Having great powers and capable of creating miracles?"

"Yes but don't forget that the power comes from a consciousness in Love and a deep trust and knowingness of who we are. With this consciousness in Love, we can create anything we desire without effort. Conversely, when we have a consciousness of Fear, we operate from the smaller aspect of Self. At this level, we become easily stressed, anxious, frustrated and angry because we are bound by the limitations of the ego and unknowingness. Do you follow?"

"Yes, Sifu."

Sifu Wang regarded the boy smilingly. "Since we are all off-springs of God, we are all linked to each other energetically and spiritually. We cannot do anything to each other without feeling the effect ourselves."

"Is that why the religious scriptures say *do unto others as you would have them do unto you?*" Hai San asked.

"Precisely." Sifu Wang nodded.

"What about trees and plants, Sifu? My friend's mother transplanted their mango tree from the ground into a pot last week. I told him it was cruel but he said his Mother said it was only a tree. So it was alright. But the tree is quite big, about six feet tall and has already started to bear some fruits."

"Trees and plants, too, have consciousness, Hai San. When we touch them with love, whether physically or energetically with our thoughts, we send them a divine energetic message directly from our hearts. The trees and plants will then spread the message of love to other trees and plants. In this way, they grow healthily and can bear more foliage, flowers and fruits. Generally, Love leads to Abundance. In the case of your friend's mango tree, it very much depends on the motivation or the intent to transplant the tree. If it was done with loving intentions, the tree would still survive well although its freedom to grow and realize its full potential had been curtailed. If the intentions had been selfish and unloving, the tree would have either died or continued to live but without bearing much fruits or become diseased. So, it's very important, Hai San, how we think, feel and act because we impact on our environment."

"Do our thoughts also affect the Earth, Sifu?"

"Yes, spiritually and energetically, our planet is linked to us. We are all One. When we think more loving thoughts, thoughts of joy, kindness, wellness or beauty, Mother Earth feels it and is positively transformed in the process. On the other hand, when we think fearful thoughts, thoughts of lack, anger, dissatisfaction or hatred, Mother Earth similarly feels it and is negatively affected. Where do you think earthquakes, drastic changes in weather patterns and diseases come from?"

"From us?"

"Yes, from us. Our thoughts and actions in totality determine the quality of our lives and our Home. We must continually honour ourselves and our surroundings with love if we are to continue living in peace and prosperity. In fact, it would be a good practice for you to start Loving and Honouring everything from now on."

Hai San frowned. "How do I do that, Sifu?"

Sifu Wang smiled. "Whenever you meet anybody, irrespective of whether you know them or not, say in your heart, *'I see the God in you. I love you.'* Can you do that?"

"Yes. It's a lovely practice, Sifu." Hai San grinned cheekily and jumped up from the sofa to bow before Sifu Wang. "Sifu, I see the God in you and I love you."

Sifu Wang threw back his head and laughed aloud. "Thank you, thank you, Hai San. I see the God in you and I love you, too."

Sifu Wang got up from his seat and hugged the boy affectionately. "Now that we understand who we all are, it's time for a little celebration. How would you like to have *dim sum* for lunch?"

"Super!"

"Good! We'll try out the new Hong Kong Restaurant at the foothills."

● ● ●

The restaurant was crowded but they managed to get a table by the window overlooking the garden. As far as the boy could see, the location of their table was about the most ideal in the whole restaurant setting and he wondered if it was pure good luck. They were served almost immediately although there were other people who had come before them. *Is it pure good luck or did Sifu apply magic here?* The boy looked around and smiled to himself.

"Help yourself, Hai San. There's oyster porridge and *cheecheong fun* as well."

"Should I honour the food too, Sifu?"

"Well, the appropriate way is to have appreciation. That means saying thank you to God for the food and to all the people who are involved in bringing it to the table. And I don't mean just the waitresses!"

Hai San grinned. Than he smiled at the small plates of buns and hors d'vres and was quiet for a while.

"I've said my thanks, Sifu."

"Good, help yourself. Ah, the oyster porridge is here." Sifu Wang thanked the waitress and handed a bowl to Hai San.

A few minutes later, with his mouth half-full, Hai San asked, "Sifu, can I ask you something?"

"Yes, Hai San, go ahead."

"Well, it's like this ... when we came in, there was a quite a crowd and no table available. But very soon, the best table became empty and we were given it, ahead of others. What's the secret?"

Sifu Wang was amused. "You're wondering whether I applied anything here. Yes, of course. And it's no secret."

Sifu Wang regarded the boy with twinkling eyes. "It's because of Love. Love is the secret. And you know it too. I've taught you. Practise it. Continue practicing it and it will well up in you. That is true happiness-bliss. When your heart is open and full with this energy, you will naturally create magic!"

Hai San's eyes shone. If love alone can do such wonders, he, too, hoped to master the art of Love one day.

SIX

THE STUDENT LEARNT TO BE POWERFUL

They were in the garden, appreciating nature after a qigong workout when Hai San asked Sifu Wang, "Sifu, how do we create prosperity?"

Sifu Wang leaned back against a rambutan tree and raised an eyebrow smilingly. "Any particular reason for asking?"

"Well...my school is organizing a lottery sale to raise funds for a new building. The first prize is a BMW Sports Series and the second is a Perodua car. I know technically we are all Gods and have creative abilities. So each of us has an equal chance to win if we each buy a lottery ticket. But how can I have a better chance than others?"

"Which are you aiming for – the BMW or the Perodua?"

"Er..first prize, of course."

"How strongly do you want it?"

"Well, it would be nice to win a BMW, isn't it?"

Sifu Wang contemplated the boy and smiled. Then he turned away. "Forget it."

"But, why, Sifu?" the boy protested, walking after his teacher.

"If your desire is lukewarm, you might as well don't waste your time. There are other better things to do," Sifu Wang threw over his shoulders.

Hai San thought for a while. Then he said, "To be honest, Sifu, the Perodua is more useful to me. It is a smaller car, easier to handle and saves on fuel. My neighbor, Aunt Patsy can drive my Grandpa around to the shops and in another two years, I can drive myself to school, the library and other extra-curricular activities."

Sifu Wang continued walking. Hai San hurried after him.

He appealed, "Sifu, will you teach me how to win the Perodua?"

Sifu Wang turned back and regarded the boy. "Are you really sure you want the Perodua?"

"Yes, Sifu."

"Ok. When is the draw?"

"30th June."

"Good, you have more than enough time to prepare yourself if you work diligently."

"What do I have to do, Sifu?"

"You have to practise being God."

Hai San's eyes rounded and he looked enquiringly at Sifu Wang.

"In the last lesson, I taught you about what it means to be God. That's only half of it. The other half will constitute today's lesson. Today, we will learn to bring the power that we have back to ourselves. This is particularly important if you want to manifest anything at all and I want you to pay special attention. Ok?"

"Ok."

"Good." Sifu Wang smiled. "Would you like to take a seat and be comfortable?"

Hai San moved a few feet to the garden table and sat on one of the seats. He then looked at Sifu Wang who took up an opposite bench.

"The history of the earth," Sifu Wang began, "for the last million years had been littered with wars, politics and manipulation of all kinds. To maintain the statusquo, the rulers and ruling class devised social hierarchies and laws to differentiate themselves from the majority and keep the latter in constant subjugation. Economics also played a big part wherein the controllers of wealth dictated the political, economic and social patterns of the day. Suffice to say, over time man became conditioned to ideas of superior-inferior positioning with their concomitant powerful-powerless attributes. The economic and social limitations experienced by man were further reinforced by his experiences of the vagaries of weather and earth movements in which he was the victim. So, for a very long time, man learnt not only to be an underdog but to cope with his underdog position.

He learnt to appease the powers that be, to follow rules and to behave in such manner as to bring about approval of others. As a result, man lost his power to external things. So the first thing we have to do now that we know we are God is to bring the power back to ourselves and to claim authority and responsibility."

"How do we do that, Sifu?"

"We must learn to operate from our heart, Hai San. When I say 'the heart', I don't mean the physical heart but the heart centre which is near the middle bottom of your chest. If you want to experience true love, true happiness and true knowledge, this is the centre you have to focus on. This is where you are connected to your Source. Now, I want you to feel the power of this centre. Breathe deeply a few times and focus on your breathing. Take as long as you like – there is no need to hurry. When your breathing has stabilized into a steady rhythm, begin to feel this area and hear your heart beat from here."

Hai San did as he was instructed and listened. After about ten minutes, he smiled.

"How do you feel?".

"Like – my heart has expanded."

"Good, you have succeeded in centering yourself. If you persist, you will feel a different energy. At times, you may want to giggle, laugh or shout out your joy. You will also feel self-confident, the kind that is unshakeable. If you practise long enough and regularly, you will reach a state where man ends and God begins. In this state, you connect to the unconscious part of you which knows no limits. You become the world and the world becomes you. Then, wonders will never cease to happen in your life."

Sifu Wang smiled across at Hai San who looked bemused and awed at this information.

"Do you follow me, Hai San?"

"Yes, Sifu. It's – so incredible!"

"Believe it and continue to practise. Whatever you desire can be yours for the asking. However, I must caution you, Hai San, that you may experience emotional upsets at the initial stages. Do you know what emotions are?"

"Yes, I think so. Confusion, sadness and anger – they are all emotions, aren't they, Sifu?"

"Yes, simply put, emotions are energies-in-motion, meaning that the energies are meant to move. However, sometimes when we experience something traumatic or sad, we hold on to the emotions and we store them somewhere in our body. The stored emotions could be energies that you have held on to from the past, be it your past lives or this life, for whatever reasons. Now in a state of relaxation, they will emerge, layer by layer, rather like an onion peel."

Sifu Wang looked at the boy earnestly. "To experience our Godself, we need to clear the stuck energies from our body. The way to go about clearing them is to feel them to the depths and breadths of your being and let them pass. If you have tears, let the tears flow. If you feel anguish, feel it fully from the heart centre until the emotion exhaust itself out. If you see any picture in your mind, let it flash through but don't, I repeat, don't – replay it or try to analyse it. Just observe. If you like, you can say, *Whatever it is, I love you and I thank you for the lesson I have learnt. I forgive you, I release you.* You got that?"

"Yes." Hai San was intrigued. This meditation on the heart appeared to be no simple matter.

"I want you to practice this meditation on your breath and heart on a daily basis. If you encounter anything unusual, let it happen naturally. You can tell me about it afterwards. If it's really something too frightening and you feel unable to cope, then stop your meditation immediately. I will guide you through it in a separate session."

"Will stopping it have any bad effects?"

"Not if you inform me immediately and I guide you through it."

"What kind of things can be so frightening, Sifu?"

"Well, who knows? Some people had frightening experiences in their past lives such as being executed to death by having their heads chopped off or they got tortured and died in extremely terrifying circumstances. So the memories of these experiences which are kept in their memory banks can emerge. Of course, some people can think things to frightening proportion without having gone through the real thing and this fear is enough to haunt them without a meditation practice. If you remember, we've all been conditioned to fear and with a creative imagination as our heritage, there is no limit to what can be frightening."

Hai San rolled his eyes and grinned to himself.

Sifu Wang raised an eyebrow. "Can I share the joke?"

"Sifu, my friend, Tim, is so afraid of ghosts he sleeps with his grandmother in the same room and never properly closes his bathroom door even in bright daylight. Everytime he has to go into the classroom by himself, he will yell out first, *is anybody inside?*"

Sifu Wang smiled. "Then you must teach him to be brave, Hai San."

"How do I teach him, Sifu?"

"Just tell him that we are all children of God. When we left Heaven to come to Earth, God gave us 3 Tools to live a Heavenly Life on Earth. The First Tool teaches us to connect to him. To have this connection, we need to assume ALL his Qualities. So every day when your friend, Tim, wakes up, he must recite all the attributes of God. Tell him to say : I AM THAT I AM. Magnificent, Glorious, Joy, Marvellously Creative, the Greatest Genius, the Grandest Provider, I AM THAT I AM, Beautiful, Omnipotent, Wonderful, Most Loving One, Most Compassionate One...I AM THAT I AM.."

"Wow! Will just saying those things resolve the fears, Sifu?"

"Yes, Hai San, when we invoke the qualities of God, we activate the Divine within us. When the Divine is activated and takes centre stage, there is no room for fear."

Hai San's eyes rounded. "What's the Second Tool, Sifu?"

"The Second Tool is the freedom of choice. Choices provide for the experiences we wish to have. If we do not choose, then we live in default and will come under the tyranny of other controlling factors."

"But, Sifu, what if we make the wrong choices? What, then?"

"Young Man, there is no right or wrong. We need to have trust in the Universe and not prematurely make judgments if things are less than perfect. Eventually things will happen as we order them even if there is some time lag or detour." However, if we do not like the outcome of our choices, then all we need to do is to choose again."

"Wow! What about the Third Tool, Sifu?"

Sifu Wang smiled and took a few deep breaths.

Hai San whistled. "Is the Third Tool our breath, Sifu?"

"Clever Man, you are absolutely right. When we breathe deeply, we connect with All that we are."

"Yippee, I'll convey to Tim these Tools when I see him tomorrow," Hai San exclaimed, so excited was he, he could hardly sit still. Then he paused, glanced at Sifu Wang and asked again, "Do they really work, Sifu?"

"Of course," Sifu Wang said, "unless your friend doesn't want to let go of his fears or his fears are so deep rooted from a past life, he needs to go through past life regression or hypnosis sessions to clear them."

"Oh! I hope it's not that serious with Tim."

"Yes, let's hope so."

SEVEN

THE STUDENT LEARNT TO PLACE AN ORDER WITH THE UNIVERSE

It was a beautiful Sunday that saw the old man and his grandson enjoying breakfast at a nearby coffee shop. The sky had never been clearer since the haze caused by the forest fires in Indonesia and the shade provided by the giant angsana trees was a great welcome to spending time outdoors. They had chosen to dine alfresco and had taken a table which was arranged outside the coffee shop.

While waiting for their meal to be served, the old man asked the boy, "So, Hai San, you have been having lessons with Sifu Wang these past two months. Have you learnt anything useful?"

Hai San broke into a smile. "Oh, yes, Grandpa! I've learnt a lot of things – the universe, ourselves, Mother Earth – and how we are all linked to and are affected by each other! Imagine, I never knew all these before."

Upon uttering the words, Hai San immediately felt guilty, remembering his commitment to Sifu Wang to keep things confidential. Then he said lamely, "There's a lot of explanation, Grandpa."

"As long as you understand and are able to follow Sifu Wang's instructions, I'm happy. The important thing is that you benefit from the teaching and are able to put your knowledge to practice."

"Yes, Grandpa. Sifu has given me a lot of practical work."

"Good," the old man replied.

Just then, the waitress came with their fried noodles. Hai San's eyes lit up with delight and he proceeded to pick up his chopsticks. Then he remembered what Sifu Wang had taught him about showing appreciation for the food. He put down his chopsticks and mentally thanked God and all the angels involved for the delicious food on the table. His grandfather, however, was oblivious to his little actions.

Hai San then picked up his chopsticks. He took a few mouthfuls of the noodles before he spoke to his grandfather again.

"Grandpa, do you remember my friend, Tim Gan?"

The old man paused with his chopsticks in mid-air. "Tim Gan – mmm – isn't he the son of the sundry shop operator?"

"That's right, Grandpa! Sifu was most kind. He taught me a method to teach Tim to be more courageous," Hai San revealed.

"Oh, really? And why does Tim need to be more courageous?" the old man asked.

"He is just so – afraid of ghosts, Grandpa."

"That is not normal." His grandfather observed. "Ghosts are actually more afraid of us."

"Oh? Why do you say that, Grandpa?"

"If you threaten them with a broom, they'll run away." His grandfather gave a crooked grin.

"Ha haha!" Hai San burst out laughing. "I'll tell Tim." His grandfather could be fun sometimes.

They ate in silence after that. As usual, Hai San ate with gusto and within minutes, his plate of fried noodles was empty.

"Do you want to order anything else?"

"Yes! I think I'll have the radish cake."

The boy waived to the waitress who came bearing a tray of steamed radish cakes. He took a plate from the waitress while his grandfather paid for it.

"Thanks, Grandpa."

"You're welcome."

And thank you, too, to God and all the beautiful souls who help to bring this delicious food to my table. I am most grateful.

Minutes later, the radish cake was also gone. Hai San drank the last drop of coffee from his cup and leaned back in his chair to observe the breakfast crowd.

Then he smiled as he recalled what Sifu Wang had said, *"Appreciate your food and the experience will multiply itself."* He had started doing that a couple of weeks ago and had since been having more free lunches and snacks of late, courtesy of his friends, aunts and uncles and of course, his grandfather.

"If you have finished," his grandfather's voice broke into his thoughts, "let's go. Your Aunt May is coming afterwards with your cousins."

"Yippee!" Hai San exclaimed with delight. His Aunt May is known for being kind as well as generous with her presents.

• • •

"Good Morning, Sifu!"

"Good Morning, Hai San! You look ready for today's lesson."

Hai San grinned. "Sifu, you said today you will teach me how to achieve my dream car."

"That's right. Did you bring your Order Book with you?"

Hai San nodded and waved his A4 sized notebook. "Is this suitable, Sifu?"

"Yes. Now, I want you to treat this as a pet project. A pet project means your favourite project, a project that you value a lot and feel happiest doing it. Every time, you open this book, you feel enthusiastic about it. Every time you think about it, you feel excited, passionate and positive about it." Sifu Wang smilingly regarded the boy and raised an eyebrow, "Can you do that?"

"Yes, Sifu."

"Good! Now you are ready to start your order with the universe."

Sifu Wang moved over to behind the table and settled into his executive chair. Then he looked across at Hai San and asked "Have you named your book yet?"

"No, I've only written my name on it, Sifu."

"Never mind, you can write it down now in big letters *'MY ORDERS WITH THE UNIVERSE'* on the front cover, above your name and sign it." Sifu Wang instructed.

The boy did exactly as he was told. "Ok, I'm done now, Sifu."

"Good. As the title of this book suggests, this is your order book with the universe. That means that whatever you want to have in life, you write it down in this book to order from the universe. The idea of putting the things down on paper is to map out your intentions. Intention is a very powerful tool, Hai San. It's telling the God Presence, *'I am serious. Get these things for me.'* Do you understand?"

"Yes, Sifu."

"At the same time, it will enable you to identify and focus on the things you really want. Otherwise, the mind will be all over the place, skimming over things on a superficial basis without depth and energy."

Sifu Wang paused and smiled. "Have you seen an order book before, Hai San?"

"No, Sifu."

Sifu Wang pulled open a drawer and took out a book and handed it to Hai San. "Take a look at this book. Tell me what you see."

Hai San flipped through the pages and noticed they were all alike in terms of organization. "They are all organized in the same way, Sifu. There is the seller's name and address, buyer's name and address, dates and product particulars."

"Good. But in your case, since we know who is ordering and who is delivering, we don't have to keep repeating it. It's already on the front cover. We dispense with the date because we don't want to limit ourselves to a certain time line. The only thing we have to specify are the items to be ordered. Now what do you notice about it?

"Mmm, they are very specific."

"That's right. They are very specific. When you want something, you don't beat about the bush. You just put it down simply and clearly so that the universe gets the right message. Can you do that?"

"Yes, Sifu. But, why can't I write down the date? The lottery has a draw date."

"Because, Hai San, we cannot be sure that is the date to be drawn. Changes can happen and extension to the deadline may be requested by the organizing committee."

"I see." Hai San nodded his head in understanding.

"Every order you place with the universe needs a summary and a detailed specification, Hai San. The summary tells the universe in one simple short positive statement the thing you see yourself having. For example, if you want a car, you say – *I have a car* or *this is my car*. If you want a house, you say – *I have a house* or *this is my house*. In other words, you say it in the present tense as if you are already in possession of the car or the house. No need to be too honest about things. Don't say, 'I don't have a car but I want one!' That would be disastrous!"

"Why, Sifu?"

"Because the universe is a field of cooperative and subjective pure potential. It takes its orders from us. If you order 'you don't have a car but you want one', you will keep 'wanting a car without getting it'. Do you understand?"

"Yes." Hai San grinned. "*I have a car.* Can I say *the Perodua is my car*?"

"Yes, you can describe it in the detailed specifications. You can also paste pictures so that you can tell a story about it."

"You may start writing the order book now, Hai San. Allocate one whole page for the one line summary so that it stands out as a clear statement of intent."

So Hai San wrote his one line summary—'*MY CAR*' on the first page.

"You may write in the detailed specifications now. Allocate, say, five to six pages for it and put a sub-title to each point you want to raise. Do you have the picture of the car?"

"Yes, I have it here." Hai San dug into his folder and took out a picture of a Perodua.

"You can paste this on and put a sub-title to it."

So Hai San pasted the picture of the Perodua car in the centre of the second page. On top of it, he wrote again, *MY CAR.*

Do you also have a photograph of yourself, Hai San?"

"Yes, Sifu. But I didn't bring it with me."

"That's ok. You can cut it out and paste it next to the car later when you're at home. It will look even better with a full sized photograph. Then, the idea looks very real, doesn't it?"

Hai San's eyes shone. The project was more interesting than he had anticipated. "Oh, yes, Sifu! It's getting very real! Thank you so much!"

"What would you like to say in the following pages, Hai San?"

"Mmm…how about 'Benefits' and 'Uses', Sifu?"

"Ok – you can write them down. But make them as positive statements of fact in the present tense. Don't say, 'I can drive it to school.' Say, 'I drive my Perodua to school'. It's also important to allocate some space to talking about your feelings about your car, Hai San. Feelings activate the energies and energies are the real stuff that make things materialize faster. Do you have any idea how to go about it?"

Hai San thought for a while and said, "I can talk about my joy, my exhilaration, my excitement on being handed the car keys. Then the feel of the steering wheel in my hands and the cushion on my back. Oh yes – and the air-cond and the soft music that flows into the car. And my school mates are cheering me as I drive through the school gates."

"Excellent! You are beginning to get the hang of it. The rule is to make your statements as simple and as clear as possible. Talk about when you use it, who your passengers are, how they all feel about riding with you, where do you drive it to, apart from your school, how do you care for it, etc. Can you do that, Hai San?"

"Yes! yes! Oh, I'm so excited, Sifu, I could burst!" Hai San exclaimed, clapping his hands.

"Good. Remember this feeling of excitement. You're going to have to supplement the order book with a lot of visualization and feelings."

Hai San widened his eyes. "There is more to do, Sifu?"

Sifu Wang chuckled. "Of course, the project is not yet complete, Hai San. Once you have finished writing your first order which is for the car, I want you to read it for a month, every morning when you wake up and every night before you go to sleep. Feel free to add on to your specifications if you feel there is more to say. After that, you can just surrender it to God to deliver it to you. I'll go through with you the visualization exercise next week together with a prayer technique."

"Thanks so much, Sifu! Shall I show you my order specifications next week?"

"Please do. It's important that you get the order right."

"What will happen if it's done wrongly, Sifu?"

"Well, it depends on the error. Many things can happen. You may not get the car or you may get it many years later and have had to pay for it. Or if you write too much about your friends enjoying it, it may go to one of them instead. So, we don't want any of these things to happen, do we?" Sifu Wang teased.

"Of course not!" Hai San grinned. Then he rubbed his head and stole a glance at Sifu Wang.

"Anything you don't understand, Hai San?"

"Well, er–Sifu, you said that when we operate from love, we can manifest anything we want. Why do I have to do all these – the order book, the prayers…?"

"Because you need to learn to focus, Hai San. You need to give attention to the things you like. Otherwise, you may end up manifesting things by default. Do you understand?"

"Yes, Sifu. Thanks a lot. It's clearer to me now." Hai San replied.

EIGHT

THE STUDENT LEARNT TO CREATE THROUGH VISUALISATION AND PRAYER

Sifu Wang leafed through the pages of Hai San's Order Book and nodded approvingly. "You've done it very well. I'm impressed."

Hai San's heart swelled with pride at the praise. "Thanks, Sifu."

Sifu Wang inclined his head smilingly and said, "With this Order Book, you now have a blueprint of your order. To bring this blueprint to live, you must give it a lot of energy and send it through a proper channel to the universe for it to manifest. Are you ready to do that today?"

"Yes, Sifu!" Hai San immediately pushed himself to sit up straighter from his favourite position on the sofa.

"Good. We will do the visualization exercise first. Do you know how to visualize?"

"Yes, it's like imagining, isn't it?"

Sifu Wang nodded. "When we visualize, we are, in fact, directing our energies to make movies in our minds. The clearer the movies, the stronger our chances of manifesting them in our lives. In your particular case, your movie is about your car. See yourself getting the car. How did you get your car? How did you feel when you got it? How did other people react? Your Grandfather – was he elated? Your friends – were they happy for you? How about your teachers? Who else was present? Start your movie now!

Remember, there's no limit to your imagination, Hai San. Give it your best shot. Cut!"

Hai San grinned. Then he breathed deeply a few times and closed his eyes. Within a few seconds, he saw in his mind's eye his school hall. His school hall was filled to the brim with people. They were the families of his school mates, his teachers, his friends, representatives of the sponsors for the prices, curious onlookers and yes, the members of the press and the public as well. His headmaster was now on stage inviting a VVIP to come up to draw the numbers for the prizes. The VVIP was led on to the stage. They started with the consolation prizes first. Various numbers were called up. Suddenly they called his number and his name. He was jolted from his seat. His friends slapped him on his shoulders and congratulated him...

"Stop, stop!" Sifu Wang interrupted.

Hai San opened his eyes in bewilderment. Sifu Wang shook his head slowly from left to right.

"Not impactful enough, Hai San. You must cut out the irrelevant parts and fast track the event to the actual announcement, otherwise you're going to have to waste a lot of time on the unnecessary issues."

Hai San ran his fingers through his hair. Where has he gone wrong? Oh, Sifu is a perfectionist!

Sifu Wang regarded him questioningly. "It's your choice – do you want to achieve results or do you just want to do it?"

"Achieve results." The boy murmured.

Sifu Wang smiled. "Good. I'll guide you through the visualization. Are you ready?"

"Yes, Sifu."

Sifu Wang spoke slowly and expressively. "First visualize the hall and all the people there. Feel their excitement and their energies vibrating higher and higher in the room as the announcements are made. Suddenly you heard the word 'Perodua' and your number and name being called out. Unassailable joy flooded your heart. Feel the energy now, Hai San." Sifu Wang paused to observe the boy. Then he continued, "You feel like laughing and shouting at the same time. You jumped with joy. Around you, your friends are rallying and yelling your name in support. The next moment you are on stage, receiving the keys to your Perodua. You say your thanks. Your heart is filled with love and gratitude. You feel so overwhelmed. You know that God has answered your prayers. Deep down you know that you are a creative being. You are dearly loved. Whatever you ask for will be given."

Sifu Wang paused for a while to let his words register. Then, he said, "Repeat this exercise a few times until you get very strong feelings about it, Hai San. You are the actor, director and producer now. The success of your movie is dependent on you."

Sifu Wang observed the boy for a few minutes. Hai San went through his visualization quietly at first. Then, he could hardly sit still. He jumped up and shout with joy. His heart had opened and sang. Pure music flooded through his veins. He wanted to announce his gratitude to the world.

Sifu Wang clapped his hands. "Well done!"

"Thanks, Sifu!" Hai San replied.

"Now you know how it's done. Work on your energies and feel the joy and love of God in your heart as you receive the prize. Run through your movie repeatedly for about fifteen minutes each session, twice daily for about thirty days. After that, keep the feeling, the knowingness that the car is yours. Trust that it will be delivered."

"What about the Order Book, Sifu?" Hai San asked. "You said to give it energy."

"Yes, as you read through your specifications, visualize each scene as vividly as you can. Feel the excitement and joy in your heart as you hold the steering wheel in your hands. Enjoy the feel of the cushions, the air-cond, the music from the stereo, etc. Visualise yourself driving with your grandfather or your friends beside you. The energy is different with each person. Can you do this exercise now?"

"How long should I focus, Sifu?" Hai San asked.

"About a minute for each specification. Just estimate, there's no need to keep looking at the clock."

"Ok."

Hai San looked through his Order Book and then closed his eyes to visualize. After about a minute, he opened his eyes and looked through his Order Book again for the next order. He repeated the process many times until he had covered all his specifications.

"I've completed my visualization exercises, Sifu."

"Good, now we come to the last part – how to say your prayers. Do you know what a prayer is, Hai San?"

"It's talking to God."

"That's right. And where is God?"

"It's within us."

"Good. After each visualization, we must say our thanks to God to confirm that we have received the object of visualisation. Do you see the sequence now – you order, then you produce and finally, you say thank you as if you've already received. Now for prayers to be effective, you must do it through your heart. I presume you have been practicing your heart meditation and breathing exercise?"

"Yes, Sifu."

"Good. Feel your energy at your heart centre like when you're doing your heart meditation. Feel gratitude there and say your thanks to God. Can you do that?"

"Yes, Sifu." Hai San nodded smilingly and proceeded to practise as instructed.

When the boy had finished, Sifu Wang said, "If you practise this method as according to what I teach you, I promise you, Hai San, you will get whatever your heart wishes."

The boy was speechless for a few seconds. Then he jumped from his seat to bow to his teacher. "Oh, thank you, thank you, Sifu!"

At last, he was getting somewhere. *Thank you God, thank you Universe.*

NINE

THE STUDENT LEARNT TO CO-CREATE WITH THE UNIVERSE

They were in Sifu Wang's living room practicing the heart meditation and breathing exercise. Much progress had been made since Sifu Wang first taught the boy the method of breathing while listening to his heartbeat. Today, they were going one step further to learn how to co-create with the universe.

"Do you remember, Hai San, that we are all connected to each other; you, I, the trees, the mountains, the rivers, Mother Earth and everything in this universe?"

"Yes, Sifu."

"Good. Because we are all connected, we influence each other via energies through our heart centres, our thoughts and our bodies. Do you know what this means, Hai San?"

Hai San shook his head.

"It means that we are never totally alone at any moment in time, Hai San. Like it or not, we have a relationship with the universe. We are all the time communicating and relating with each other; giving our energies to, and receiving energies from, each other."

"Oh, Sifu, what happens if we receive energies from people who don't like us?"

"It depends on whether you accept or reject the energies."

"But, Sifu, how do we know that the energies have been directed at us?"

"We won't know, Hai San, as long as we don't wake up to be conscious beings. That's why it's important to be awake. When we are awake, we become very powerful. Our love energies can touch and positively transmute the negative energies of others. And our hearts will always tell us everything we need to know to keep us safe, happy and well provided. But if we are not yet fully awake, we will not know when we are receiving negative energies until we feel weighed down, depressed and dis-eased. To get ourselves back to normal, we need to go back to our core, breathe and vibrate ourselves back to a higher frequency. However, the purpose of today's lesson is not to learn about all these. It's to teach you to co-create."

Sifu Wang looked at Hai San smilingly. "What do you understand by the term *co-create*?"

Hai San thought for a few seconds and said, "Create together with somebody?"

"That's right! You seek the assistance of another and jointly create. What I want you to be aware of is that we, humans, are not the only beings on earth. There are angels, spirit guides and various divinities with God consciousness around us, keeping us company, giving us advice and inspiring us to reach our own magnificence. When we are in need of help, we don't always have to just rely on ourselves. We can seek the assistance of such divinities. Isn't that nice?" Sifu Wang said cheerfully.

Hai San frowned. "Are these spirits *ghosts*?"

Sifu Wang laughed. "No, not at all."

Hai San managed a tremulous smile. "Then what are they, Sifu?"

"They are Gods like us except that they have made the decision not to take human birth. Some of them had been human beings before and had become enlightened. Now they are in spirit form, helping us to reach our higher purpose. Others have never taken human birth at all but are in spirit form all the same, helping us to ascend and to live a more divine creative life on this planet. We are all One Family, Hai San. We are all offsprings of the God Source. Just as you would assist a family member requiring assistance, so too would they assist us when we ask for help. There is no need to be afraid of them, Hai San, *ever*."

As if to prove his point, Sifu Wang used a classic example. "Jesus Christ, too, was from the same family of light, a God no less but was born a human. He was an extraordinary human because he didn't have limitations like most of us. He proved his godliness through his ability to command the elements and perform miracles. Now he is available in spirit form to assist us." Sifu Wang looked quizzically at Hai San and snapped his fingers. "When Christians are in trouble, what do they say?"

Hai San grinned. "Jesus, help me!"

"That's right. Or *God, help me!* In the same manner, when Buddhists face a challenge, what do they say? *Namo TassaBhagavatoArahatoSamma Sambuddhasa* – or *Om Mani Padme hum* or something similar. It's the same concept, Hai San, except that we expand the usage to a whole lot of things and we can request assistance from any relevant divinity, not just Jesus Christ, Buddha or Siva. When you need help from a friend, say, Tim Gan, what do you do?"

"I'll call him and ask him to help out."

"Exactly. It's the same thing. We all live in a co-dependent world and if we can ask another to help us out, everything in life becomes simpler."

Sifu Wang regarded the boy smilingly. "Are you comfortable with it now, Hai San?"

"Yes, Sifu, but when should we co-create?"

"When we need to achieve a specific objective and it's easier to seek another's help. Look, I'll tell you my own experience when I was a young man. I was residing in KL then and driving to the Subang International Airport one morning when I met with the most horrendous traffic congestion. At that time, KLIA was not built yet. My flight was scheduled to depart at 8.45 for Penang and here I was, right in the middle of a traffic that wouldn't move and with only forty-five minutes left to take-off. What could I do? I didn't have much knowledge then about the things I know now. But I knew one thing – desperation. I had to get on the flight because I had an important meeting in Penang. So I appealed to God. All the way from PJ through the Subang exit to the airport, I was talking to God to let me take the flight. When I reached the airport, there was only five minutes left to take-off. Guess what happened, Hai San?"

"You managed to get your seat!"

"Yes! Not only that, the plane developed a puncture on one tyre and the flight had to be delayed by half an hour while they put in a replacement. In normal circumstances, they wouldn't have let me got on the plane."

"So weren't you late for your meeting, Sifu?"

"No, I was just on time. But it was a harrowing experience. I had another similar one two years later. But, that's quite a long story."

"Oh, please tell me, Sifu." Hai San begged.

Sifu Wang smiled, remembering that the boy loved to hear stories. "Alright."

He leaned back in his seat and stared into the distance as he recalled. "I was preparing to depart for Madras from a private hangar at Subang International Airport one morning. As a Consultant, I'd brought with me the original papers for presentation to a business associate in India. The documents were placed in a briefcase which were stowed near the front passenger seat where I sat. When I got out of the taxi, my colleague was calling me to assist him with his bags. I went to the boot to help out and before I knew it, my colleague had paid the taxi driver and the latter had driven off with my briefcase. I panicked, of course. I couldn't let my client knew that I had fouled up. So what could I do? Apart from calling the taxi company to radio the taxi driver to return, I prayed to God for help. We were scheduled to fly by private jet and departure time had been fixed. When we reached the ground handling office, however, the pilot delivered his bombshell – the flight had to be delayed.

What's the problem? – my client demanded.

The battery is flat, Sir – the pilot answered.

Didn't you check the night before? – my client queried.

We checked everything, Sir, and it was perfect. I couldn't believe it myself when the battery went flat half an hour ago.

So, what now? – my client demanded.

So, now we have to wait for the aviation engineers to come back from their breakfast to re-charge the battery – the pilot replied.

How long will that take? – my client asked.

The engineers will be back in half an hour's time but the battery will take about three hours to re-charge, Sir. All in all, three and a half hours, Sir – the pilot concluded.

My client fumed while I laughed inside. God had answered my prayers! A load was lifted off from my mind. And true enough, the taxi driver returned on time with my briefcase. I paid him the full fare but it was worth it."

"Sifu, wasn't it a dangerous thing for tyres to get punctured and batteries to go flat?"

"In the ordinary circumstances, yes, I would say it's dangerous if it were not discovered on time. But you have to remember, Hai San, I didn't plan it all. God did and what God does is always perfect. There are no errors in God's world."

"Since God is so reliable, if I co-create, can I just talk to God and not to any other divinity?"

"Yes, Hai San. But there will come a time when you will find that it's relevant and meaningful to seek specific divinities for specific problems. It's more efficient to be *focussed*, Hai San. We're all in God's family."

"How do we know that an entity is a God, Sifu?"

"Gods are characterized by Love and Light. When your senses are strong and sensitive enough, you will see flashes of light when they're near. Their energies are of very high frequencies and have potential to heal. Know that they're your friends and you're never alone."

"I see."

"If you're ever in doubt, Hai San, always ask, *Dear One, are you from the Light? If not, stay away.* Anything other than Light will depart because you are God and your words have power. Do you understand, Hai San?"

"Yes."

"Good.

"What do we say when we want to co-create, Sifu?"

"*Well, it depends on what you want to co-create. When my briefcase was being driven away in the taxi, I said to God, 'God, I have an important presentation. I need my papers. Please get the taxi man to come back with my briefcase on time before I take off.'*"

"It's that simple, Sifu?"

"Yes. Some things in life are really very simple, Hai San. It's all a matter of trust. God has given us the tools to co-create with him. But first, we must have trust and confidence in ourselves and in Him that it can be done. That trust and confidence must come from inside of ourselves. Without that, it's all lip service."

"Sifu, the other day when I was in a school bus about to reach home, it started to rain. I didn't have an umbrella with me. So I got wet. In this situation, can I co-create to ask for the rain to stop for a few minutes for me to reach home so that I wouldn't get wet?" Hai San asked.

Sifu Wang roared with laughter. "What's a few drops of water, Hai San? So, get wet! Rain is good for you."

Hai San grinned. But he persisted in an appealing tone. "Can I co-create for the rain to stop, Sifu?"

"Yes, of course," Sifu Wang confirmed.

"What should I say?" Hai San asked.

"What do you want to say?" Sifu Wang teased.

"How about *'God, I don't want to get wet. Please stop the rain for a while?'*" Hai San replied, then started to laugh himself at the ridiculous request.

Sifu Wang roared with laughter again.

Finally, he said, *"Just say, 'Oh Divinity in charge of the weather! I don't have an umbrella with me. In another ten minutes I'll be reaching my home. Please stop the rain for five minutes then so that I can reach my home dry. Thank you, Divinity in charge of the weather! Repeat until the rain stops. You got that?"*

"Yes, Sifu. Thanks." Hai San grinned.

TEN

THE STUDENT SUCCESSFULLY PRACTISED CO-CREATION

Tim Gan leaned against a casuarina tree and regarded his friend, Hai San, solemnly.

"So, what are you going to do? You can't report him to the Principal, can you?" Tim was asking.

"That's the whole problem. Fran didn't dare to complain. So, who am I to report it? Besides, he's smart enough to pretend that nothing's happened."

"But he's taking it out on you. It's not fair! The whole class was surprised when he made those derogatory remarks about your ability. Then he had the audacity to challenge you to give him front page news! And they're national papers no less, not any mere school magazines! The man is mad."

They were in the school compound discussing the latest unfriendly behaviour of their Form Teacher, Anthony J, who just a couple of weeks ago was found by Hai San to be making a pass at a female student. Without the victim's cooperation to report to the school principal, Hai San could do nothing. But the damage was done. His presence as a witness to the sordid incident had seemingly turned against him. Suddenly, he was target number one for the teacher's cruel and taunting remarks. It was as if by challenging the boy in this manner, the threat of being exposed would be significantly reduced.

Hai San gestured frustratedly. "What else can I do?"

Tim considered the question silently. Then he said, "Anthony J never used to be like that. But I heard he's had a bad time after divorcing his wife. Maybe it's a passing phase."

"Well, it doesn't help my current position, Tim. I cannot let him get away with his bullying. As the Form Teacher, his appraisal in my school report card carries weight. I've got to do something before he spoils my future altogether."

"Mmm. Do you think speaking to another teacher will help?"

"I doubt it, Tim. This matter is kind of – sensitive. Nobody will want to get involved. Consider it my bad luck!" Hai San gave a grimace.

"Well, sleep on it! Maybe, tomorrow things will be better." Tim gave Hai San an encouraging pat on the shoulder.

"I can only hope," Hai San said, without conviction.

Before they got on their bicycles, Hai San reached out to the trunk of the casuarina tree. Tim looked on in surprise. "What're you doing?"

"Just to say, *Cheers,* Buddy!"

Tim shook his head. He couldn't understand what his friend was about. Things weren't so bad after all if his friend could still say *Cheers.*

. . .

Two days later...

"So, what's up, Hai San? You sounded desperate when you called me earlier."

Hai San stopped his pacing and looked at Sifu Wang. "Sifu, I'm in trouble – real trouble."

His voice almost broke.

"Hey, sit down first. No problem is so bad that it cannot be resolved. You want a drink? I'll get Maria to fix you a fruit punch."

Hai San just shook his head. He couldn't think of anything else while the matter of the media challenge and his irate Form Teacher remained uppermost in his mind. He dropped down heavily onto the nearest settee.

Sifu Wang came back and sat opposite to him. "Tell me what's wrong."

"It's my Form Teacher. About two weeks ago, I happened to step into my class during break time and found him with a female student. He was – he had his arm round her – " Hai San's voice trailed away.

"You caught him making a pass at her."

"Yes. But it's what's happening now that makes things difficult. He's – he's out to make trouble for me, Sifu. Every day he picks on me at the least opportunity and – and he makes fun of me to the whole class. I can take his taunts up to a certain limit, Sifu – but when it comes to my school work and appraisal, I cannot let his unfair treatment continue. Now we have a school project in which we are assessed and our marks are recorded as part of the overall score for the final examination. It is this matter that I am worried about," Hai San said.

"What's the name of your teacher?"

"Anthony J."

"Roughly how old is he?"

"Er, about forty-five."

"Mmm." Sifu Wang was silent for a while as if in meditation. Then he smiled as if amused.

He looked at Hai San. "It's ok, Hai San. He's not going to be a major problem. What's this project that you have to do?"

Just then, there was a knock on the door and the housekeeper came in with a tray of drinks.

"It's an environmental awareness project, Sifu. We have to design questionnaires and go out and survey the level of environmental awareness amongst the residents of our neighbourhood. The class is divided into eight teams. We've already completed our survey and analysed the results. Now, each of the teams has had to prepare a report."

"Thanks, Maria." Sifu Wang took a glass of fruit punch and passed it to Hai San. "So, what's so difficult about it?" he asked Hai San.

Hai San gulped down his drink. "Well, apart from working together as a team, each person in the team has a specific role and he is awarded marks based on how well he performs that role and how good a team player he is. I'm supposed to prepare the report and I've already done that, Sifu. But, it's not enough." Hai San stared down miserably at his drink.

"Go on."

"Anthony J says anybody can prepare a report. He's given me a new assignment – I've to prepare a Press Release for the whole class and get the media to cover this project. He says he wants front page news in the New

Straits Times and the Star. My appraisal will be based solely on that. I'm the only one assigned to do this, Sifu. The others don't have to do it at all."

"What's the worst thing that will happen if you don't get front page coverage?"

"Get lower marks."

"Did he say that?"

"He implied it, Sifu."

"He doesn't have the courage to carry out his threat, Hai San. And he doesn't think you'll be able to get front page coverage, anyway. But, you can always surprise him, can't you?"

"Sifu! You mean – it's possible?" Hai San's eyes shone all of a sudden.

"Of course, Hai San. Have confidence. With the tools I've given you, you're a powerful person now."

Hai San started to smile. "Which method should I use, Sifu?"

"Which method do you think is appropriate?"

"Mmm. Let me think – visualize?"

"I don't think you have enough time, Hai San. When's the news coverage expected?"

"Next week. I've to arrange for the press conference by next Tuesday."

"No problem. You have a relationship with the universe, don't you? Use it."

"Co-create, you mean? Ah – why didn't I think of that earlier?" Hai San grinned. It was amazing how useful the technique can be. A life-saver. Oh, what a shock it will be to Anthony J!

Sifu Wang shook his head. "Don't harbour any thoughts of revenge, Hai San. I know your ego has been bruised and you want your pound of flesh back. But, anything that is based on the ego doesn't work. If you want things to work, you need to be sincere right here." Sifu Wang pointed to his own heart. "You got that?"

"Yes, Sifu." Hai San sobered down immediately.

"If anything, after all you've been through, you have a right to prove your capability. Call for the divinities in charge of the press and get their assistance in full earnestness. This will be a good practice of co-creation for you," Sifu Wang said.

Hai San smiled in relief. "Thanks a lot, Sifu. I feel better already."

• • •

Tuesday morning came. The sun shone brightly as if to signify a great day ahead and the sky had never been bluer. At SMS Methodist, waves of excitement could be felt. As early as 8.30, the whole school was agog with news that a press conference was going to be held. It was the first time that such an event had been organised and it was no wonder that the school grapevine was working overtime.

Headmaster Joseph de Silva who had been informed the day before was, nevertheless, taken by surprise to see a whole team of reporters trudging into the school hall together with their photographers. Hai San's team, despite anticipating a good turnout from the media, was unprepared to receive as many as two dozen press representatives. Though they had enough press kits to distribute around, they did not have enough chairs and had to quickly borrow from the nearest classroom.

Anthony J was in his element. Transformed suddenly into a mini-celebrity, he managed to hold court with the reporters for almost an hour, fielding questions like a pro and permitting Hai San and his classmates opportunities to answer only when detailed results of the survey were specifically asked.

When the last of the press representatives left, there were all smiles and the class of Form 4A heaved a big sigh of relief. Everybody concurred that the event was a huge success. Anthony J, however, could not resist a parting shot at Hai San with his warning reminder, *'See that it's front page news'.*

Some of Hai San's classmates who heard the parting shot gave Hai San a sympathetic look. Though they were puzzled by their Form Teacher's recent treatment of their classmate, they were not daring enough to offer any assistance.

Hurt by the reminder and the silent pitying looks, Hai San breathed in deeply a few times to calm himself. His consolation at this point was that his practice of co-creation had worked! The press conference had turned out exceedingly well and even Anthony J couldn't fault him. Now the only thing left to do was to get the front page news which was no mean feat. But Sifu Wang had been confident and had not thought that it was an impossible task. Sifu's encouraging words – *'Have confidence – you are a powerful person now'* – seemed to echo in his heart.

Yes, that's right. I'm a powerful Being, a God no less. Oh, Divinities in charge of the Press, get me front page coverage in all major newspapers. Thanks a lot!

ELEVEN

THE STUDENT LEARNT TO MANAGE A DIFFICULT PERSONALITY

As Sifu Wang had anticipated, the coverage on the school project appeared in the front page headlines in the major newspapers. It became a one week wonder as the whole school of SMS Methodist glowed with pride and busied themselves over the unprecedented attention it received from members of the public. The headmaster Joseph de Silva was never more pleased. At the school assembly two days later he publicly commended Anthony J and the class of Form 4A for their environmental awareness study and the outstanding coverage in the press. Anthony J took the credit in his stride and so did the entire class.

As for Hai San, he now knew with absolute certainty the truth of Sifu Wang's teachings – they're powerful and awesome. So were all his divine friends. He decided that he would devote more time from then on to practise what Sifu had taught him. Although he had been practicing them quite regularly, it was not with the fervour that he should have in view of competing interests for his time, except during the last week when he had been pushed into a corner by Anthony J.

Overall, the publicity and ensuing excitement had served to mellow the Form Teacher's attitude towards the boy to some extent, but not fully. Once every few days, he would issue his challenges and wait mockingly to see if the boy would rise to his bait. Weary from all these unnecessary pettiness, Hai San decided to seek Sifu Wang's advice again.

"Sifu, do you still remember my Form Teacher, Anthony J?" the boy asked Sifu Wang one day.

"Yes, Hai San. Is he still giving you trouble?"

"Yes, Sifu."

"How serious?"

"Well, they're not really serious, not like the school project. But his taunting can be wearisome and stressful."

"If they're stressful to you, then they're serious. Do you know that your health can be affected by stress?" Sifu Wang studied the boy.

"I didn't realize it could be that bad, Sifu. Every time he gave me a bad experience, I recovered by doing my breathing exercises and positively motivating myself back to normal."

"You can't keep doing that all the time, Hai San. It would be no different from a frog jumping two feet up a well to fall back two feet or worse, three feet," Sifu Wang said. He looked at Hai San in the eye and said cheerfully, "We need to teach the *bastard* a lesson, don't we?"

Hai San's eyes rounded with surprise, then he laughed. He felt his heart lifted. "You're joking, Sifu!"

Sifu Wang let out a guffaw.

"Of course. You were getting lost amidst all your jitters. You're a God, Hai San. All the power is within your being. Always remember that. When you encounter the little hiccups in life, you deal with them in a divine way."

Hai San frowned. "But, how?"

Sifu Wang gave the boy an amused look. "Get a pen and paper," he instructed.

Hai San excitedly dug into his bag for his stationery. Then he looked at Sifu Wang expectantly.

"Write a letter to Anthony J and talk to him heart-to-heart."

"What! How can I?" Hai San was aghast.

"Just do it." Sifu Wang was firm. "Tell him – tell him with the authority of one who is a God – to stop his pettiness and his unfair treatment. Tell him how you have worked to maintain his integrity and to achieve a name for him and the school. Tell him that he doesn't have to be a tyrant –

because you're not a victim. Above all, tell him to get rid of his own guilt and his own emotional punishment. You deserve to be a free person and so does he. Can you do that?"

"Yes, Sifu. Er, what happens if he doesn't like it?"

"We'll deal with that later."

"Ok."

So the boy got to work. Very soon, one page was not enough. He took out another sheet and then another sheet and continued writing. He poured out his heart and soul – six weeks of heart-kept anguish, all laid bare to be addressed by Anthony J. When he had finished, he felt relieved, as if the whole episode was behind him.

Sifu Wang looked at him questioningly, "Finished?"

"Yes."

"Now crumble the letter and throw it away."

"What!"

"You heard me."

"But, Sifu, I've just spend one whole hour writing the longest letter of my life!"

"I assure you, Hai San, if you had written it from your heart as I've taught you, it's not wasted. Trust that his soul has received your message. You are now both free to move on," Sifu Wang said.

• • •

Incredibly, from that day onwards Hai San witnessed a change in his Form Teacher's behaviour. From a personality that was constantly sarcastic and threatening to Hai San, he was now an epitome of charm and good behaviour. It was as if the whole unfortunate episode had never happened.

Hai San was intrigued. He asked Sifu Wang how this could possibly happen.

"Communication, Hai San. Communication is the key. When you operate from your godself, your words which are sincere goes out and touch the other person's heart. A miracle then happens. Nobody is beyond redemption, Hai San. But sometimes it takes a slightly longer time to change a person. If a person's agenda this lifetime is that of a good person, the change will be quite fast. Anthony J obviously belongs to this category."

Hai San was further intrigued by this new knowledge. Agenda? Sifu had never mentioned it before.

"Sifu, what if a person's agenda is that of a murderer, a thief or a scoundrel?"

"Then, he will play the role to his satisfaction until he tires of it and wants a change. You see, Hai San, even before a person is born, he has already decided the kind of life he will have on earth, who his parents, his siblings, his teachers, his friends and his enemies will be and what they will do to enable him to experience certain kind of life circumstances. Nothing happens by accident, Hai San. Everything is by our choice. We all made our choice before we were born. But even then, a murderer, a thief or a scoundrel is not one all the time."

"What is the purpose of all that agenda, Sifu?"

"If you remember your first lesson, Hai San, we are all individuations of the God source. Father-Mother God desires to know of Itself and experience Itself fully. But It has no means of experiencing Itself unless It creates something which It is not, to differentiate. So It creates this world of illusion. In tandem with the grand agenda, each soul chooses its own mini agenda in which to experience itself.

Hai San frowned. "What if we decide we don't like our agenda half way through?"

"Then we change it."

"Are we allowed to do that?"

"Of course, Hai San. We are the producer, the director and the actor. We can do anything we like. There are no limitations."

"How do we know what is our agenda, Sifu?"

"We don't know the full agenda, Hai San. When we enter into illusion, we enter into forgetfulness of who we are and what we have planned. The only thing we know is that what gives us *passion* is part of our agenda. Every event in our life is a moving piece of story we bring into it. If we know our full agenda, then everything in life becomes static and uninteresting. We would all be like robots, wouldn't we?"

"Yes, life's more interesting because we don't know what's coming on. It's the guessing, the anticipating and the living it that create excitement."

"Precisely. Life is just a game, an adventure. If we forget this point, then we have missed the objective of living altogether."

TWELVE

THE STUDENT LEARNT ABOUT DISEASES AND HOW TO HEAL

Hai San parked his bicycle under a mango tree and walked wearily up the driveway to Sifu Wang's house.

Before he could raise his hand to ring the doorbell, Maria, the housekeeper, opened the door. "Good afternoon, Hai San. Sifu asked you to meet him in the Orchid House."

"Good afternoon, Maria. Thanks, I'll make my way there myself." Hai San walked to the side of the two storey bungalow and climbed down a few steps to a conservatory where more than a dozen variety of orchids grew in wild abundance. Despite its name, the conservatory also housed a few other varieties of plants which Sifu Wang had brought back from his jungle trips with the Forestry Research people.

Sifu Wang looked up from his examination of a seedling and cheerfully smiled at Hai San as the boy approached.

"Good afternoon, Sifu."

"Good afternoon, Hai San. Why are you looking so down today?"

"It's nothing." Hai San denied, hands in his pockets, still looking glum.

"Nothing? Can nothing change a handsome face to one that looks like it's received a funeral notice?" Sifu Wang lightly queried.

Hai San was startled. *Surely Sifu was not predicting anything!*

"Sorry, Sifu," he admitted. "I – it's just some bad news about my friend's mother. She's got liver cancer."

Sifu Wang regarded the boy silently. Finally, he said, "You look shaken, Hai San. There's nothing to fear, really. Diseases is part and parcel of life, don't you know?"

"Yes, Sifu. But in this case, we're talking of cancer, not just cough and cold. People experience a lot of pain and they die."

"Not necessarily," Sifu Wang said and he put down his seedlings into a planter box. He looked at Hai San quizzically. "Do you know how diseases happen, Hai San?"

"Well, some diseases are caused by germs and some by toxic accumulation in the body," Hai San replied.

"Partly true. But why is it that some people get them and some don't?"

"Some people have stronger resistance. Maybe it's also in the genes."

"You are quite right. However, I want you to understand one thing. Fundamentally, diseases happen because there is imbalance in the energy system in our body. Diseases are wake-up calls, Hai San. They tell us when things are not right with the way we have been living our life," Sifu Wang explained.

"Oh, does that mean that my friend's mother is not living her life in the right way?"

"Yes, but put it like that, it sounds terrible, doesn't it? I don't mean to sound patronising." Sifu Wang smiled and walked over to a garden bench. He sat with his arms stretched out, looking relaxed. He looked at Hai San who had perched himself on a sculptured limestone rock and continued. "The reality is that we are all made up of energies. Energies need to be constantly moving and circulating, Hai San. A perfect blueprint of health is where our energies move harmoniously and in a balanced manner in alignment with our inner truth. That's when our body cells not only get nourished with fresh vital energy and oxygen but are cleansed off the waste products such as carbon dioxide and uric acid. Conversely, when imbalance occurs in the body due to conflict within ourselves, it sets up a blockage or blockages within the body. The cells stop getting their nourishment and the waste products start to build up. We then have a condition we call dis-ease. That means the energy in our bodies is not moving with ease."

"Is that all? It sounds so simple, Sifu. What about the diseases that are passed through the genes?"

"Well, every person brings with him his own personal agenda when he is born. That agenda is recorded in the DNA. A soul who decides to experience a certain life circumstance such as a disease will choose to be born in a family which has the potential for the disease to happen. But it doesn't mean that everything that is recorded in the DNA will materialize, Hai San. Whatever is recorded there remains a potentiality until it is activated by certain factors or events leading to stress, grief, continuous holding on to negative issues and the like. Disease is merely a choice, Hai San, for the negative aspects of life until the person decides that he has had enough."

"And then what happens, Sifu?"

"Love happens. The person changes his emotional matrix from fear to love. If he gives an intention or a strong wish for change, events will occur in his life to facilitate his recovery."

Hai San scrambled down from his perch on the limestone structure and walked a few steps to stand before Sifu Wang. "How can we help my friend's mother, Sifu?"

Sifu Wang smiled indulgently at the boy. "You'll have to ask your friend's mother whether she'll accept alternative therapy. Otherwise, *no go*."

"If she does?"

"Then you fix us the appointment."

"Thanks, Sifu!" Hai San beamed.

Yippee! Sifu was going to heal his friend's mother.

• • •

The appointment was fixed for nine o clock Saturday morning. Hai San was up at Sifu Wang's place as early as eight o'clock. As soon as he had parked his bicycle, Maria opened the door and came out carrying a basket of fruits and vegetables.

"Good Morning, Maria!" Hai San called out cheerfully.

"Good Morning, Hai San. You're early today!" replied the housekeeper.

"Yes," Hai San replied. He peered into the contents of the basket. "What's this?"

"Fruits and vegetables. Sifu asked to load them into the car."

"Here, let me help you." Hai San took the basket from Maria and bent down to lower the basket onto the back seat of the Mercedes.

"First time I've seen vegetables given as a gift." Hai San declared.

Sifu Wang laughed from behind. "You have to learn, don't you?"

"Oh, I'm learning, I'm learning," Hai San grinned cheerfully. "Why vegetables, Sifu?"

"Not just any vegetables, Hai San. Those are rich in potassium."

"What's so special about potassium?" the boy asked, his interest piqued.

Sifu Wang smiled. "It facilitates the cancer cells to revert to normal."

Hai San's eyes rounded. "How come the doctors never told their patients?"

"I can't answer for them, Hai San. Maybe they do." Sifu Wang replied.

"Or maybe they don't," Hai San concluded simply.

"Come, Hai San. We've got to go. I need to pick up something on the way."

"Ok, Sifu."

• • •

Sifu Wang sat opposite the patient with Hai San beside him while Hai San's friend, Ken Chye, hovered behind his Mother.

"Madam," Sifu Wang began slowly as if preparing the patient for what was to come, "there is a lot of repressed anger here – " he pointed to his own torso to indicate where the liver is, "which is causing you the dis-ease. You need to clear this stuck energy, otherwise your problem may worsen."

Then he leaned back in his chair and regarded the patient compassionately. "Whoever and whatever they may be, can you not forgive and move on?" Madam Tang gave a gasp and attempted to deny. But after one look at Sifu's face, her own crumbled and she started to sob.

"Mum, it's ok, don't cry," Ken Chye tried to console his mother.

"What – would you know – of a woman's feelings, Kenny?" she continued to sob. So deep was her distress that she sobbed for a full five minutes. Ken Chye plied his mother with tissue paper while Sifu Wang looked on with compassion. Hai San sat immobile, hardly daring to breathe. Finally, Madam Tang calmed down, blew her nose and gave a weak smile of embarassment. "Sorry, I can't help feeling emotional," she said.

Sifu Wang nodded in understanding. "It's good to clear your emotions."

"Sixteen years – Sifu – sixteen years of being regarded as the disadvantaged daughter-in-law – with no money and little education. Oh – the problems my-in-laws gave me! It got worse after – after my husband died. How can I forget, much less forgive?"

Sifu Wang said gently, "I've no doubt that you've suffered, Madam. However, the way to get over a bad experience is not to keep holding it but to feel it fully and understand its significance for learning. Every experience we have is always an opportunity for us to remember more about ourselves and to change what we don't like about our situation. Your children are still young and depending on you for support. Would you forsake them just to nurture your anger?"

Madam Tang was silent for a while. Then with a firm resolve, she said, "No, my children are all I have. I'll change, I'll change, Sifu!"

"Good," Sifu Wang approved. "For healing to be really effective, you must make a conscious decision to change. Otherwise, I can't create miracles!"

Madam Tang managed a slight smile. "How will you heal me, Sifu?"

"I will need to clear the blockage and balance your energies by working on your chakras," Sifu Wang said. "Chakras are energy vortexes in our body which can pull in energy from the universe to assist our body functions. I will begin by opening and activating your chakras so that they will spin more effectively. I will also channel energy into your affected organ to expedite your healing."

"How long will this – *chakra* healing – take, Sifu?"

"About two to three minutes per session per day."

"Wouldn't it – be a waste of time to travel all the way for only a few minutes of healing?"

Sifu Wang smilingly shook his head. "Madam, I do my healing by *remote*, meaning that I don't have to be physically present but can still channel the energies to you."

Madam Tang appeared to consider the explanation. Then she asked, "Is that all?"

"No, I want you to actively participate in your own healing process. Will you do it?"

"What am I required to do, Sifu?"

"You need to change your thoughts and feelings about yourself. Practise self love more often and be at peace with yourself and others.

All of us are formed of love energy, Madam. Our body cells need love everyday to survive. That's why when we hold on to negative energies such as anger and withhold love, the body gets dis-eased. I'll teach you a new way of looking at things."

Madam Tang looked sad but she nodded. "For my children, I'll try."

"Good, good," Sifu Wang encouraged.

"Also try to eliminate animal meat, milk and highly processed foods from your diet, at least for a year. Take more fresh fruits and vegetables, particularly those with high potassium content. I've included them in here," Sifu Wang continued, indicating the basket of fruits and vegetables at the side table.

Hai San went over to the basket and took out a few items to show, which included beet root, pumpkin, starfruit and banana.

"Thanks, Hai San," Sifu Wang acknowledged and added, "Lemon is also good for your liver."

"It would be good if you could also practise qigong on a daily basis to increase your oxygen intake and to move the energy in your body. We have a qigong expert here who can teach you," Sifu Wang said, patting Hai San affectionately on the shoulder.

Hai San felt a rush of pleasure and offered, "Anytime you're free, Auntie."

"Thank you, Hai San, that's kind of you," Madam Tang replied.

Sifu Wang took a sweeping look at his surroundings and suggested apologetically, "Maybe you could do a thorough cleansing of your home as well, Madam."

"Does my home look that dirty?" Madam Tang asked, somewhat affronted.

Sifu Wang laughed lightly. "The energy here is a bit dense. To enjoy better luck and relationships, Madam, you need to have a free flow of fresh energy. I suggest that you get your children to help you clear out your old things and do some spring cleaning."

Madam Tang averted her gaze while she tried to assimilate this new information. "I see. How long will it take for me to recover, Sifu?"

"It depends on you, Madam. Only you can decide how fast you will heal."

"If I want to heal within, say, three to four months, can it be done?"

"Of course," Sifu Wang assured her.

Looking visibly relieved, Madam Tang asked, "Do I still need to go for surgery and chemotherapy, Sifu?"

"What would it achieve?"

"I – really don't know. Many people have continued to live and many have also died in great pain."

"*Dis-ease* is just a wake-up call to us, Madam, to re-examine ourselves, our values, our thoughts and our lifestyle so that we will bring about changes to ourselves to achieve *ease*. The people who recovered and lived healthily on took this call positively and they made wonderful changes in their lives. The rest who died, didn't. Rest assured, if you decide to make a positive change, whichever treatment you undertake, you will survive. It's your choice – you decide."

Madam Tang was silent while she contemplated her options. Then she asked, "When can we start my healing?"

"I can do the chakra healing for you now."

"Alright, what do I have to do, Sifu?"

"Just relax – I'll open your chakras first."

Everybody refrained from talking while they watched Sifu Wang concentrate on channeling the energy to Madam Tang. After about a minute, he smiled and said, "Ok, Madam. Your chakras are now opened and spinning well. If you can, concentrate on your crown chakra," he pointed at the top of his head, "for about five minutes each day. It will help you recover a lot faster."

"Thank you, Sifu ...er, what about the other methods?"

Sifu Wang shook his head. "Get a rest first, change your diet, clean the house. We'll go through the other methods on another day."

"Sifu, ...how should I pay you?"

Sifu Wang smiled charmingly. "I heard you're a great cook. When you're recovered, I hope you can treat both Hai San and I to a sumptious dinner!"

Madam Tang's eyes lit up and she looked relieved. "Of course, thank you, thank you so much, Sifu!"

"Thank you, Sifu," Ken Chye echoed. He thumped Hai San on the back gratefully, "Thanks, Hai San! I owe you."

"Glad to be of assistance, Buddy! I hope your mother recovers fast," Hai San replied.

THIRTEEN

THE STUDENT LEARNT THE KEYS TO HEALTH, HAPPINESS AND ABUNDANCE

"Today, I am going to teach you on how to heal the chakras," Sifu Wang said. He turned to his white board and drew a diagram of a human body. Then he marked out seven circles on the body and labeled them with various names.

"It is important to know about chakras because chakras deal with light energy and we are all light beings – Gods," he said. "Do you recall our earlier lessons, Hai San, that we are all from the Family of Light?"

"Yes, Sifu."

"Good. Our body is designed to hold, capture and transmit light. The capturing and transmission of light is done via the chakras. *Chakra* is a sanskrit word meaning disc or wheel. When the chakras spin, they look like discs or wheels, like this." Sifu Wang drew another diagram on the board. "There are many chakras on our body and some outside of it. But for our purpose, we will deal only with the seven major chakras on our body, namely the Crown Chakra, Third Eye Chakra, Throat Chakra, Heart Chakra, Solar Plexus Chakra, Sacral Chakra and Root Chakra," he said, pointing to the respective position of each chakra.

"To have good health," Sifu Wang continued, "our chakras should spin all the time and in a balanced manner. But this is easier said than done. The lack of knowledge regarding ourselves and the challenges of living in an illusionary world can affect us to the extent that we become lost within the dramas that we have created. Instead of releasing our emotions fully, we repress them. Instead of living spontaneously from the heart, we live bound by the limitations of the ego. In this way, we create blockages and stress within our energy systems which eventually develop into dis-eases. The role of a healer, then, is to harness light into the system so that the chakras will begin to spin well, blockages will get cleared and stresses eliminated.

"A healer is a facilitator then, Sifu?"

"Absolutely. Nobody can heal a patient unless the patient wants to be healed," Sifu Wang said. "I am going to open six of your chakras for you in stages so that you will be able to work with energies and do simple healing as and when required."

"Oh, thank you, Sifu! But, why only six, and not all seven chakras?" Hai San excitedly asked, immediately curious.

"The energy at the root chakra is our life-force, Hai San. It is very strong. If we don't know how to control it, it will blow us up. Yogis have died trying to manipulate this energy and some have become paralysed. That's why it should not be prematurely opened. When you're ready, it will open by itself naturally." Sifu Wang explained, his voice serious.

"Oh." Hai San looked dazed at the information.

"Ok, sit up straight and relax. I'll open your chakras now."

Hai San immediately sat up straight and looked at Sifu Wang expectantly.

Sifu Wang was silent as he concentrated on opening the energy centres on Hai San. After a few minutes, he smiled in a satisfied manner and said, "Ok, they're opened now. I want you to close your eyes, breathe in through your nose and breathe out through your mouth a few times, then focus on your crown chakra for about ten minutes. When you're done, take a few deep breaths again."

Hai San started to follow Sifu Wang's instructions but he felt sensations all around his body. He couldn't determine exactly which point they were coming from. He started to fidget.

"Relax – take it easy," Sifu Wang instructed. "Just feel the energy. I'll help you to balance it."

After ten minutes, Hai San took a few deep breaths and opened his eyes.

"How do you feel?" Sifu Wang asked him.

"I feel lighter, Sifu. But there is a certain pressure on my head."

"It's a kind of suction feel, isn't it?"

"Yes, that's right."

"That's ok. Your crown chakra is beginning to pull in energy from the universe. You'll get used to it." Sifu Wang regarded the boy smilingly.

Hai San smiled back, eyes shining and feeling very excited now that his chakras had been opened. The only thing left for him now was to learn how to heal.

"Healing is pretty simple, Hai San," Sifu Wang said as if he had read his thoughts. "Always remember that you don't use your own energy. You are just a channel for the divine healing energy to come through. You bring in the energy through your crown chakra by concentrating on it. The energy then goes to your hands. So you place your hands on the chakra points of your healee, the person you want to heal and transmit the energies through. At any one time, your hands can be on two, three or four chakra points like this," Sifu Wang demonstrated on the diagram.

"How long should we place our hands on the chakras, Sifu?"

"About one to two minutes for each placing but not more than five minutes per session of healing. If you feel a back flow on your fingers, stop healing immediately."

"Why, Sifu?"

"Because when the healee's had enough, he will stop accepting the energy. The energy will then flow back to you. You will need to stop, otherwise you own energy circulation may be disrupted and you may fall sick yourself."

"Oh, I see."

"If a healee has pain in a specific area, we can additionally place one hand on the affected area and the other hand on the corresponding chakra, like this," Sifu Wang demonstrated. He turned to check whether the boy was following him. "Anything you don't understand, Hai San?"

Hai San gave a sheepish smile, "Sifu, why is it that you didn't use your hands when you were healing Madam Tang?"

Sifu Wang laughed, amused at the boy's thoughts. "It's not necessary for me to. At an advanced level, we can channel the energy by just pure intention. You will one day also learn to do it this way. But for now, you have to use your hands."

"Ok," Hai San grinned. A feeling of excitement coursed through his body. He couldn't believe it – *he's going to be a healer!*

"Have you fixed the next appointment with Madam Tang?"

"Yes, Sifu, next Saturday, same time."

"Good. I want you to meditate on your crown chakra for at least five minutes everyday. When you go there, you can practise healing on your friend."

"Yippee!" Hai San exclaimed happily. Then he stopped short. "But, Sifu, Ken Chye is not sick!"

"No, but he had a headache the other day which I brought down. If he continues to worry about his mother, he is likely to get migraine soon."

"Oh!" Hai San was astonished. *How did Sifu know? Ken Chye never complained.*

"When we're there, you might as well teach Ken Chye and his mother the qigong exercises I taught you."

"Lifting the Sky and Carrying the Moon?"

"Yes and include the warming-up exercises as well."

"Ok, Sifu!" Hai San smiled with pleasure and rubbed his hands together. He couldn't wait for Saturday to come – and start healing his friend.

• • •

They were at Ken Chye's home at nine am the next Saturday.

The qigong session with Hai San went on well and lasted almost an hour. Thereafter, Hai San did healing on his friend under the watchful eye of Sifu Wang.

"I'm impressed, Sifu, with your methods. It's been just a week since we met up and already, I'm feeling better," Madam Tang confided.

Sifu Wang laughed happily. "I see you have followed my advice. The energy in your home is different and you are accepting changes. That is great. You see, all of life is about living our truth, the truth of what we are. There are only two major options; to be with the truth or to be against the truth. When we are receptive to truth, there is no resistance and we enjoy ease, good health, happiness and abundance. But every time we are in denial and resistance to truth, we set up conflict within our aura, thereby attracting the same into our life. The trick to living happily is to live with our hearts open and in full consciousness and alignment with our inner truth. In that way, we always have *flow*. But that is easier said than done, eh?

"Yes, this is what I'm afraid of – Sifu – that I will be negative again and revert to feeling angry, inadequate and worthless because they are treating me this way."

"My dear, you need to learn to love yourself. Nobody can make you feel less than what you are unless you allow yourself to be so."

Madam Tang was silent as she tried to register the information. "How can I love myself more, Sifu?"

"That is a billion dollar question," Sifu Wang chuckled. "Accept and appreciate yourself as you are, without reservations, guilt or apology. Know that you are unique in this world and that you have your own path which is different from anybody else's, so don't compare yourself with any standards outside of yourself. Don't even look to anybody else for validation. Everything you need and want is really within you – follow your heart, your own guidance – when something crops up, ask yourself 'Is this me? Do I need it?' It is ultimately your own experience that counts, not somebody else's interpretation. When you live your life valuing your own truth and principles without criticizing or judging others, you are paving the way for other people to accept you as you are. Loving self involves feeling good about oneself, caring for oneself and honouring oneself without needing to be perfect."

"Isn't that being self-centred, Sifu?"

"Self-centred – yes – but not selfish. We all come into this world to write our own story and star in our own movie. This is our primary responsibility. When we can care for ourselves, we will automatically take care of the world."

"It requires a lot of courage to be that – assertive. I'm not used to it and I'm not sure if I'm too late to start."

"No one is ever late, my dear. The power is within you all the time, waiting to be expressed. It is a matter of choosing whether you want to honour the other person or yourself. The minute you decide to honour yourself and give it attention, your energy configuration changes and you will be given every assistance in the universe to follow your truth. But should you decide to honour the other person at your own expense, you will set up blocks and stresses in your own body because you are acting against your personal truth. Think about that. Which path would you follow?"

Madam Tang remained quiet but her heart thumped with excitement. Sifu sounds so steady, so knowledgeable and reassuring. It was true – she had allowed herself to become a doormat over the years because she had valued other people's opinions more than her own. She had forgotten to love and care for herself. No wonder her body rebelled. "I'll follow my own personal truth," she finally declared, smiling shyly.

"That's great!" Sifu Wang's smile broadened.

"We've finished our healing, Sifu." Hai San announced.

"Good. Take a break." Sifu Wang advised. The two boys flopped down onto nearby chairs while Madam Tang excused herself to go into the house for drinks. Sifu Wang looked at Ken Chye and asked. "Are you feeling better now, Ken Chye?"

"Oh yes! Thanks, Sifu." Ken Chye grinned. "How did you know I'd been having headaches?"

Sifu Wang smiled and said, "We are all One. I couldn't have come within three meters of any of you without feeling what you are feeling."

"Wouldn't that be tough on you if all of us were in pain, Sifu?" Hai San asked jokingly.

"Not at all. I can choose not to be affected."

Wow! Both boys silently breathed.

They took a break for fifteen minutes, drinking a concoction of fruit juices which Madam Tang had prepared and talking about things in general. Then it was time to proceed to the next session.

"I'm going to teach you the secret to a happier life," Sifu Wang began.

Everybody came to full attention.

Suddenly, Hai San's voice rang out. "Sifu, please excuse me. I need to go to the washroom."

"Ok, five minutes." Sifu Wang smiled.

"Hei, friend, you can only have one minute – don't keep us waiting." Ken Chye gave a mischevious grin.

Everybody laughed. Hai San turned back to make a face before he rushed towards the house. Then he came back in record time. Everybody laughed again.

"Ready?" Sifu Wang asked.

Hai San grinned. "Yes, Sifu."

"Good. What I want to specifically impart is that we are all Beings with varying levels of consciousness. This consciousness sits within our aura and creates its own stories with the input we give to it. Depending on what we feed it, we create our experiences."

"How does that happen, Sifu?" Ken Chye asked.

"The external universe mirrors what we hold in our aura."

"I say, Sifu, does it then follow that if we want more money, we should think of having money more often?" Ken Chye asked.

Sifu Wang laughed. "Logically, yes. But money by itself does not have any significance to our inner being. It is what money does ultimately to our feeling of self that is important. Ask yourself: *What is it really that gives me joy, peace, comfort and a sense of fulfillment?* This is what your inner being is after and this is what you will magnetise faster. So, open your options – there are unlimited ways of getting what you want and money is only one of the avenues."

For a few seconds, the group was bemused. To be told that money was not the only means to achieve one's desires and objectives definitely required some mental adjustment.

"Alright! I know what I want!" Ken Chye's voice broke the silence. "I'll go for the Perodua!"

"Hei, Buddy! That's mine!" Hai San protested.

"Best man wins!" Ken Chye declared, raising both his hands.

"Let us see!" Hai San mockingly threatened.

Sifu Wang and Madam Tang looked on in amusement.

• • •

On the way back, Hai San asked, "Sifu, do you think Ken Chye's mother will recover?"

"There is no reason for her not to. She has improved tremendously within just one week and if she is fully focused to change her attitude, she will recover."

"Wow, that would be a miracle!" Hai San exclaimed.

Sifu Wang chuckled. "Yes, but only to people who do not know how the world operates. How do you think Jesus healed the sick?"

"Well, he – used his godly powers."

"Yes, his own energy automatically balanced the energy of the sick and he knew them as whole and perfect, being the Gods they are. In reality, there is no reason for any of us to be sick or even poor or unhappy because that is not our real heritage. But the illusions of this world can be very convincing. In order not to be caught, we need to continually tune in to our God Self."

"Which is accessed through our hearts." Hai San added.

"Yes." Sifu Wang smiled. His student had certainly learnt well from him. He turned his head slightly and asked, "The school holidays will be coming soon, won't they?"

"Yes, next weekend. I'm looking forward to them."

"That's good. Enjoy yourself – go camping, dating or whatever you boys do at your age. The world is made for living."

Hai San laughed. "I will, Sifu. Thank you – for everything."

"My pleasure." Sifu Wang turned his head and smiled at the boy. "I'll see you when school reopens."

FOURTEEN

REUNION

Hai San was in a dilemma. He didn't know whether to continue laughing or to break down and cry. The school lottery was finally selling, after months of inactivity. How it had happened, nobody knew. It was as if some magician had waved a wand over the new building site during the school vacation. And hey presto, like football fever, nobody could get enough of it. To say that Hai San was shocked by the response, was not totally correct. When he heard the first bit of grapevine on the school lottery, he had thrown back his head and laughed headily, in great relief. It was purely reactionary for one who had loved his alma mater and all that it stood for. But, as the morning wore on, he began to have his mis-givings. Not that he begrudged his alma mater the success it deserved for its building fund but that the sudden mass enthusiasm and excitement of a thousand over students with equally high hopes of winning the top three prizes was alarming enough to throw any sane contender out of his comfort zone. Hai San alternated between feeling glad and fearful. Glad because congestion in the classroom was about to become a thing of the past. Fearful because he perceived his own chances of securing the Perodua becoming slimmer by the hour. By mid-morning, his own internal conflict was building up into a dullness in his head. A dullness he couldn't seem to shake off, even when he focused on his Crown Chakra. He felt like he was moving towards a huge void, with no goal in sight.

"Bring your power back, Hai San." His teacher's voice seemed to call to him from a distance. "Bring your power back."

A heavy hand landed on his shoulders. Hai San jerked out of his meditative state.

"Hei, Hai San! Where were you?" his friend, Tim Gan, asked in amusement.

Hai San turned to his friend and gave a sheepish grin. "Nowhere. What's the update, Tim?"

"God Almighty – Benjamin's father has bought him two hundred tickets as a birthday gift. And Fran's just bought another fifty and Siew Mei, thirty."

"What?" Hai San choked over his words.

"One ticket for each family member," Tim Gan enunciated.

"No kidding?"

Tim Gan laughed and shrugged. "That's what they say." He surveyed the school hall and then looked testily at his friend. "Not going to increase your stake?"

Hai San grimaced. He shot a look at his friend. "Will it make *any* difference?"

"You never know, Buddy. It just might!" Tim Gan replied cheerfully. "I'm going to buy another ten." He quirked a brow. "Join me?"

"I – " Hai San was about to make some excuses when his attention was caught by some commotion at the far end of the hall. He stopped to observe the scene curiously. Tim Gan followed his gaze. Several of their school mates were crowding excitedly around one of the school's top students.

"Hah – what's our Number One Bookworm doing?" Tim Gan asked sardonically, folding his arms and viewing the scene with narrowed eyes. "He's acting like he's discovered some hidden treasure."

Hai San flashed his friend an amused look. Trust Tim Gan to say it exactly as it is. "Let's go take a look."

They walked briskly towards the scene. As they approached the excited group of students, Hai San's heart started to pound. His whole body went cold.

"Hei, what's the book he's holding?" Tim Gan gestured at the group leader.

Hai San stared at the person in question with disbelief. Then he turned to his friend and answered without expression, "It's *The Flying Star Fortune Tips*."

Tim Gan whistled and shook his head. "Looks like they're bent on winning."

Hai San shrugged. With feigned nonchalance, he turned away from the scene. The dullness in his head was starting to climb back in. He was at his wit's end. Never before had he felt so *shaken and disturbed*. Oh, what should he do? What should he do? He drew in a deep breath. How *could* he simply compete with so many people? *How?* He drew in another deep breath. And another. Suddenly, everything became clear and calm. *Sifu!* Yes, that's it – he would visit Sifu after school. Sifu would surely have a solution for him.

Beside him, Tim Gan was secretly grinning as he took out his own wallet to count his remaining currency.

• • •

"Sifu!" Hai San called out, momentarily forgetting his worries upon seeing his teacher at the Orchid House. "Sifu, it's so good to see you again!" he beamed. Now that he was on familiar ground, he could feel some of his tension easing away. There was something different about the air in and around Sifu's house that redeemed one's sense of balance and focus. He had definitely lost all focus today.

"Great to see you, Hai San!" Sifu Wang beamed back, holding out his arms in welcome. They hugged affectionately, as a teacher would with his favourite student. Then the older man pulled back to look into the eyes of the younger one. "There's nervous energy in you, young man," he observed, eyes twinkling. "What's up? You can't be nervous coming back here!"

Hai San laughed in relief. *Trust Sifu to know instantly!*

"Of course not,' he declared, "It's just that I was a bit unsettled by some news in school today."

"A bit unsettled, huh? I would say –very unsettled," Sifu Wang teasingly corrected. "Come," he said, motioning for the boy to follow him. He took off his slippers and left them at the foot of a limestone sculpture. Hai San widened his eyes in surprise at his teacher's actions but immediately took off his own sandals as well.

"Let's take a walk to calm down your nerves," his teacher said.

Hai San eagerly fell into step with Sifu Wang.

"Breathe," his teacher instructed. "Breathe as deeply as you can."

Hai San began to breathe deeply, in-out, in-out, in-out… Soon he had a rhythm to it. His teacher observed and nodded approvingly.

"Now, place your attention at the mid-point of the soles of your feet. Feel them connecting with Mother Earth."

Hai San brought his attention down to his feet and walked reverently a few steps to get the feel of being connected.

"Feel yourself sinking or melting into Mother Earth as you walk," Sifu Wang instructed.

"Yes, Sifu," Hai San replied.

"Good." His teacher commented after a while.

They walked at a relaxed pace in meditative silence for about five minutes. Then Sifu Wang said, "Now, feel yourself sinking further downwards, to two to three feet underground."

Hai San felt himself sinking downwards.

"Are you there now?" his teacher asked.

"Yes."

"Good."

They continued walking in meditative silence for about ten minutes. Then Sifu Wang said, "Now, imagine your whole body sinking and melting into the heart of Mother Earth."

Hai San took a few deep breaths and felt himself sliding further downwards and melting into the core of Mother Earth.

This time round, Sifu Wang didn't ask him any question. He observed his pupil for a few seconds before continuing to walk in silence. Hai San, too, walked in silence. He continued to breathe – in-out, in-out, in-out…. And he walked. Feeling himself embraced in the Heart of Mother Earth. Loving her. Being loved in return. Feeling Supported. Feeling Nurtured. Step after step….. Breath after breath….., he continued – in-out – in-out – in-out. Then *something* moved, blossomed, inside of him. A feeling of Joy. Happiness. He started to giggle.

Sifu Wang's laughter rang out in full gusto.

Hai San's giggles gave way to full laughter.

The two males having fun in the garden?

Maria, the housekeeper, looked out through the kitchen window curiously and grinned to herself at the vision she saw – an older man and a boy were alternately throwing back their heads and doubling up a number of times in what looked like an extremely hilarious private joke between them.

She shook her head, hummed to herself and resumed her cooking.

"How do you feel now?" Sifu Wang asked the boy after the initial mirth had slided away.

"Oh, I feel *great*, Sifu!"

Sifu Wang grinned at the boy. "What you have just gone through, Hai San, is called 'grounding'. Grounding is an important exercise to connect us with Mother Earth. Being humans, Gods that we are, we have a foot in the spiritual realm and a foot in the material realm. Mother Earth is our Guardian Angel in the material realm. She nurtures us, takes care of us in all aspects of our material life. So, we need to be constantly in touch with her. When we are in touch with her, we feel stabilised, focussed and confident and we are able to carry out our work in a balanced manner. If you ever feel down, disorientated, anxious or afraid again, be sure to do your grounding exercise to regain your balance."

"I will, Sifu," Hai San replied happily.

"Good. Now that we've both been nurtured by Mother Earth, shall we say our thanks?" Sifu Wang reminded Hai San gently.

"Oh, yes!" Hai San nodded eagerly.

Both teacher and student stood in reverence for a few seconds to say their thanks to Mother Earth.

When they had finished, Sifu Wang turned to Hai San and suggested with a twinkle in his eyes, "Maria will have prepared us some refreshments. Let's go and get it."

"Super!" Hai San exclaimed, all his worries apparently over.

They walked back to the limestone sculpture where they had left their shoes and true enough, there was a table laid nearby. Sifu Wang went over and lifted off the food cover. "Mmm. Smells good," he said smilingly and motioned for Hai San to take a seat. "Please, help yourself, Hai San. These fritters are still warm from the *kuali*."

Hai San sat down eagerly and beamed at his teacher. "Thanks, Sifu. They look great!"

"Maria makes one of the best *pisang goreng* in Air Itam," Sifu Wang commented and handed Hai San a cup of Ipoh Coffee. "Try the *ubi goreng* as well." He set the plate down in front of Hai San.

Hai San beamed. "Thanks, Sifu." He took a piece and inwardly thanked the Divinities of food for the abundance. Then he bit into it experimentally. The crispy coating crackled and Hai San's eyes widened as his teeth encountered the softer filling inside. "Mmm, yum, yum, this is deli-cious," he declared. He took another bite and another bite, closing his eyes to savour the taste.

Sifu Wang looked on at the younger man's obvious pleasure with delight. It was not often that people had as much appreciation for food as his student did. He helped himself to a piece of *pisang goreng*. "So, what's the news that you heard in school today?" he asked conversationally.

"My school mates are buying our school lottery by the fifties and hundreds, Sifu. Some have combined forces to buy in bulk to improve their chances of winning..." Hai San tried to explain but his voice tailed off as he noted his teacher's amused expression.

"Good for them, good for your school," his teacher merely commented.

Hai San looked down at his plate. All of a sudden, his uncertainties began to surface. How could Sifu say that? *What about him? What about his Perodua?*

"How many did you buy?" Sifu Wang asked, eyes twinkling.

Hai San looked up and smiled sheepishly. "I bought another ten today."

Sifu Wang threw back his head and laughed. "That's good. That's charity, Hai San."

"Oh, Sifu, You don't think it's necessary, do you?"

"Of course, it's necessary. The school needs the funds. How else is it going to finance its new building?" Sifu Wang reasoned.

"But, but – you don't think it's necessary to buy extra tickets to win the prize?" Hai San stammered.

"To win the prize, no," Sifu Wang shook his head, eyes crinkling. "Not necessary at all."

The student absorbed the information in dismay.

"So – I was carried away by the tide of events," he admitted after a while.

"Then bring your power back," Sifu Wang replied matter of factly.

Hai San felt a jolt of energy shooting up his back. That's what he heard this morning! But then, saying it or hearing it was easier than getting it done. He thought wistfully. How *many* times had he tried to calm himself down but to no avail? He needed to be a Master like Sifu to be able to control himself at will.

"Sifu," Hai San began in a small voice, staring down unhappily at his plate, "the competition is too great. Some of my school mates are consulting geomancy to enhance their luck."

"Really?" Sifu Wang raised his brows in surprise and his mouth quirked in amusement before he drank his coffee. After he had drunk his fill, he leant back in his chair and declared, "Competition is just an illusion, Hai San. And consulting geomancy to win is just wishful endeavour. Forget about them. I'll teach you something more worthwhile."

Hai San perked up. Excitement laced through him. The fears of the morning faded into the background.

Sifu Wang observed him and asked, "Do you remember what I taught you about inputting the things you want into your aura?"

"Yes, Sifu," Hai San replied.

"Good. That's the only thing you ever need to form your reality. What other people do or say is of no consequence. If your friends want to buy a thousand tickets, let them. If they want to consult the best geomancer in the world, so be it. It should not affect you. Nothing other people do need affect you."

"It needn't? But, *why*, Sifu?" Hai San was curious.

"You are a God, remember?" Sifu Wang smiled at his pupil. "You have all the capabilities of creation within you. So, why should you worry or for that matter, shake in your shoes, if other people choose to do what they want? You please yourself and you let them please themselves. *Alright?*"

"Alright, Sifu."

"Good. I'll re-visit the subject matter of our *aura* in our next lesson," Sifu Wang promised. "You'll need to fully understand its significance if you are to master the art of manifestation."

Hai San's eyes lit up.

"Have another cup of coffee," Sifu Wang offered.

"Thanks, Sifu," Hai San gratefully accepted another cup. He took a few sips and then ventured carefully, "Do you think I stand a good chance of winning the Perodua, Sifu?"

Sifu Wang looked at Hai San in amusement. "It's not what *I* think but what *you* believe," he replied.

"Huh?" Hai San's eyes widened as he gulped down a mouthful of coffee.

"Never mind, I'll go through with you on Saturday. It's a big subject matter and cannot be hurried," Sifu Wang said with a smile.

FIFTEEN

THE STUDENT LEARNT ABOUT THE PERSONAL UNIVERSE

"The *aura* is just a convenient word," the teacher smilingly admitted as he sat back in his garden seat. "I used it because that's the word most people understand. And it is also easier to conceptualise. But, what I really meant was our *Personal Universe*. Our *Personal Universe* is vast; larger than what most of us have imagined. Can you take a guess how big our Personal Universe is, Hai San?"

Hai San recalled the feeling he had every time he enters the compound of Sifu Wang's house. Maybe Sifu's Personal Universe is the size of his house. "Is it the size of this house?" he ventured.

Sifu Wang raised one brow in surprise. "No."

"I mean, including the garden?"

"No," Sifu Wang was amused.

"How about three houses of this size and the gardens put together?"

"I'm afraid not," Sifu Wang chuckled.

"Ten houses and their gardens then!"

Sifu Wang roared with laughter. Hai San frowned, scratching his head. He couldn't imagine the Personal Universe bigger than ten sprawling bungalows with their equally large gardens.

"Then how large is our Personal Universe, Sifu?" he asked humbly.

Sifu Wang gave his pupil a wide grin before he dropped his bombshell. "Our *Personal Universe* extends to the core of the Earth, the far reaches of the Universes and beyond, across Dimensions. Our Personal

Universe is who We Are. Or rather, We Are our Personal Universe. We are in IT and IT is in US. We are, potentially, Everywhere."

Huh? Hai San scratched his head, frowned and stole a glance at Sifu Wang. *Universes? Dimensions? Has Sifu gone overboard this time?* But his teacher remained nonchalant, leaning back in his garden chair and smiling with great satisfaction as he breathed in the fresh morning air slightly scented with freshly cut grass. Hai San frowned down at the earth doubtfully and then leaned backwards in his garden seat to raise his head heavenward. He squinted against the glare of the mid-morning sky through the pattern of mango leaves above him and quickly lowered his head as his eyes began to water. He blinked rapidly. Undeterred, he gave his teacher a lopsided grin and asked, "Sifu, if we are almost everywhere, where is there space to fit everybody?"

"Good question!" His teacher looked at him with approval. "To understand, Hai San, you need to place yourself out of Duality. When you stand outside of Duality, Everything is infinite. And Space becomes an illusionary concept, applicable only in linear time. We are, how should I say – holograms, yes, holograms of All That Is. That means, we are each a part of the whole and also the whole. We are the Universe or should I say, the Universe is in Us. Yet, at the same time, we are a part of IT as well. Can you grasp what I am saying, Young Man?

Hai San felt a warming in his heart. He liked the idea of Sifu calling him a Young Man.

"Yes – I think so. But it's – complex," Hai San replied cautiously.

Sifu Wang nodded his head in understanding. "It requires standing outside of our Self to truly grasp the concept. We can do an experiment on holograms one of these days, if you like. Then you will understand better. Now, coming back to our Personal Universe, what is it really? Do you have any idea?"

Hai San shook his head.

"It's our Repertoire of all of ourselves in our sojourn through illusion. It contains every concept we've ever had about ourselves, every thought, feeling, belief, idea, habit, behavioral pattern, experience, relationship, you name it. They're in our Personal Universe. Every time we think, feel and conclude in a certain way, our thoughts and feelings are recorded in our Personal Universe."

"But, Sifu, how is this relevant to manifesting our dreams?" Hai San asked in earnest.

"Another good question!" Sifu Wang commended with a smile.

"There is a cosmic law relating to balance, Hai San. Everything in the universe is subject to balance. Balance is what keeps the sun, the stars and the planets in their place. It is *the factor* that maintains the on-going Creative Process. The Law of Balance ensures that what we put into our Personal Universe is what we will get in our life. In other words, the universe at large will always *mirror* back what we programmed into our Personal Universe. So, if you want something to manifest in your life, all you have to do is to ACTIVATE that thing that you want in your Personal Universe."

Hai San frowned and contemplated this as he leaned back in his chair. *It's all so bizarre. So Out of the Ordinary.* He caught a whiff of some fragrance in the air. He sniffed and smiled appreciatively.

"Does it really work?" he asked his teacher.

"Of course." Sifu Wang smiled fondly.

Hai San sniffed again. He had recognised the scent by now – a mixture of rose and cinnamon or something. He had smelled it many times before when he was with his teacher and he had been puzzled by it but had not wanted to ask anything so personal. Finally, curiosity had got the better of him and he had asked Maria in confidence where the scent had come from. Maria had at first laughed aloud and her belly had shaken uncontrollably with mirth. Finally, she had revealed that the scent had come from Sifu Wang.

Hai San looked at Sifu Wang and asked, "Is that the reason why you taught me to visualize, Sifu?"

Sifu Wang nodded. "Precisely. But visualization doesn't cover it all. It's the Choice, the Intent, behind it and the Feeling, the Imagination and the Breath that get things activated."

"Lots of people don't achieve their goals," Hai San commented.

"Mmm, that's because they have ambivalent ideas about them," Sifu Wang responded. "They may have, at one time or another, thought about something they wanted. But, simultaneously, they also harbour thoughts of not wanting them for certain reasons. Or their past programming controls them to such a degree that they resist the idea of owning those things they desire. It's a very funny thing, Hai San, how people carry their conflicting ideas. And funnier still is that they are unaware of it."

Hai San frowned. *Has he been ambivalent towards winning the lottery? Does he hold any resistance within him to owning the car?*

Sifu Wang continued, "It's a common occurrence, Hai San. To manifest, we can only have *one dominant idea* about the thing we want to manifest and we need only *love ourselves* to have it. There is no need to hold any agenda regarding it. Just *love* yourself, then *release* and allow your Breath to bring in the *Balance*."

"But, Sifu, what happens if other people come along? Is there any way we can stop them?"

Sifu Wang shook his head. "No, and there is no need to bother either." He looked intently but kindly at his student. "Other people's actions and behaviour are their own personal free choices and they will always move in and out of our life as according to their choices and in response to our energy and our feelings and thoughts about them. To the extent that we are affected by them, to that extent is the *mirror* telling us what it is in our Personal Universe that we need to address."

Hai San hung down his head in silence. He felt his throat tighten up and his eyes began to water. Blinking rapidly, he took a few deep breaths and admitted in a small voice, "I have resistance within me, Sifu."

Sifu Wang nodded in understanding and waited patiently for his student to continue. Seconds seemed to pass.

"I'm afraid," Hai San said, lifting up his head to look at his teacher. "I'm afraid I may not win the Perodua."

Sifu Wang leaned back in his seat and looked at his student with sympathy. "Why? Because other people have more tickets than you?"

Hai San nodded miserably.

"Where's the logic? Nothing has changed," Sifu Wang calmly pointed out. "You're still pitted against the same number of tickets."

Hai San frowned, trying to get what his teacher was saying. "But they have more tickets, Sifu. It's easier to strike a prize if you own more," he reasoned.

"Nothing doing," Sifu Wang was firm. "What do they have?" he gestured smilingly. "Only pieces of paper. It's the idea, the Consciousness of Who You are in relation to this thing that you want, that counts. You must assume your Sovereignty, Hai San. Real Winners know how to sit quietly at the Centre of their Personal Universe and *allow* the Law of Balance to manifest for them."

He watched his student intently for a few seconds. "I have an idea. Give me a ticket," Sifu Wang said.

Hai San searched into his wallet and took out the ten that he bought that morning.

"Just one will do," Sifu Wang said.

"Which one?"

"Any one."

Hai San selected one ticket and handed to Sifu Wang.

"Thanks, Hai San." Sifu Wang then shove his hands into the pocket of his trousers and drew out a couple of ringgit notes and handed them to Hai San.

"Oh, Sifu, it's ok." Hai San was reluctant to accept the payment.

"Take it, Hai San. I'm buying it."

"Why, Sifu?"

"Because I want to." Sifu Wang smiled.

"But you already have a Merc, Sifu." Hai San was puzzled.

"So, couldn't I have another car?"

"Er, of course, Sifu." Hai San flushed.

Sifu Wang chuckled and gave Hai San a pat on the shoulders. "Don't worry, Young Man. There will be plentiful opportunities for you. But, first, you need to sort out your fears and doubts. You have made a giant out of them and given them the importance they should not have."

"Yes, Sifu, but *how*?" Hai San pleaded. "How should I deal with them?"

His teacher smiled and replied, "Easy, Hai San. Just breathe. Breathe your fears and doubts gently into the core of your Being. You know how to do that, don't you?"

Hai San shook his head. "It's difficult, Sifu. I – I feel so challenged," he admitted.

Sifu Wang gazed at his student with compassion. *The boy needs to make peace with his Personal Demons, alright.*

"You have to be patient, Hai San. The accumulated beliefs and misperceptions of many lifetimes cannot be cleared in a few sessions. It will take months or years." Sifu Wang admonished.

"But – but – the lottery draw will be in a couple of months' time!" Hai San's voice cracked in panic.

"There will be other opportunities, Young Man," Sifu Wang calmly placated. "Believe me, when you have mastered yourself, the World will be your Oyster. When that time comes, there will be nothing that you can't have if you really want it."

SIXTEEN

THE STUDENT LEARNT TO ACCESS HIS OWN PERSONAL UNIVERSE

You have made a giant out of your fears and doubts.
The accumulated beliefs and mis-perceptions of many lifetimes cannot be cleared in a few sessions. It will take months or years.
Believe me, when you have mastered yourself, the World will be your Oyster.
There will be nothing that you can't have if you really want it.
Sifu's voice seemed to echo in his head.

● ● ●

Hai San pressed on the door bell and stepped back. He smiled with anticipation as he thought about what he was going to learn in the next couple of hours. Though the revelation last Monday was a real downer on his mood for it meant that he had a lot more work to do on himself before he reached his goal, he had decided that it was all for the best. At least, now he knew what kind of obstructions he had placed within himself. Sifu Wang had said that he had made a giant out of his fears and doubts but that the underlying cause was his past programming. So, great – Sifu was going to teach him to clear himself of his past issues.

Hai San whistled as he waited. He heard a shuffling of feet from inside and before he knew it, the door was opened. Maria was all wreathed in smiles. "Hello, Hai San! Come on in."

"Hi, Maria. How are you?" Hai San grinned back at her.

"Fine, fine. And you?"

"I'm very well, thanks, Maria."

"That's good, that's good." The housekeeper closed the door and led the way in. After a few steps, she turned back to Hai San with a smile and gestured to the left. "Sifu is in there. Go on in," she urged.

Hai San grinned at Maria and tip-toed across the hall to the Meditation Room which was located in the north-east corner of the sprawling bungalow. He opened the door with caution and peeped in. Sifu Wang appeared deep in meditation.

He crept in quietly and took his seat a few meters away. He drew in a few deep breaths. Oh, the air is so wonderful! A fresh floral fragrance – something like jasmine. He breathed in his fill appreciatively and felt his heart opening up.

"Ready for today's lesson?" Sifu's voice floated to him.

"Er, yes, Sifu." Hai San turned to his teacher and smiled.

"Good." Sifu Wang stretched a bit and leaned back. "Let's take a refresher first on the Personal Universe to see whether you've understood it correctly. What can you tell me about your Personal Universe?"

Hai San sat still and tried to recall what his teacher had taught him the week before. "My Personal Universe is *me*," he began, "it contains everything that I feel, think, believe and experience. It is very large and extends almost everywhere. It contains my past issues and – er – my present and – er- my future?" He looked towards his teacher hopefully for confirmation.

Sifu Wang lifted his eyebrows, "Hmm, go on."

"Well, it's just me, all of me, I guess."

"That's right," Sifu Wang affirmed with a smile. "Your Personal Universe holds the story of you and most importantly, your awareness and your relationship with yourself and others, the beliefs you hold, the attitude you take and the choices you make with regard to things that happen in your life. It contains the directions, the potentials and the probabilities for your future as well. So, if you don't like what you are receiving in life right now, all you need is to change your beliefs, your attitude and the choices that you have made."

"So, *how* do you create and manifest things in your life?" Sifu Wang questioned.

"Through our breathing, what we hold in our Personal Universe will be activated and mirrored back as experiences in our life," Hai San replied.

"Good, good." Sifu Wang nodded approvingly. "So, if somebody were to come and knock you down, who created the thought for it to happen in the first place?"

Hai San was silent as he pondered this issue. Based on what Sifu had taught, *he* created it, *didn't he? But, who is so stupid as to create his own accident?* He looked at Sifu Wang and replied tentatively, "I did?"

Sifu Wang laughed. "You don't sound very sure, Hai San. But you're right. We are responsible. Much as we would like to blame it on the other person, the fact is: if we are knocked down, it is because we have created an idea in our Personal Universe for the experience to happen."

"Sifu, why should we want to create an accident of all things?"

"There could be numerous reasons, Hai San. One of them is the personal urge for retribution, to right a perceived wrong that we've done onto others. Some others could be a wake-up call that we've placed within ourselves in order to bring us back on course with our Life Agenda. But we will go into that later. Right now, I just want you to remember that there are no mistakes in life. Everything that happens to us happens because we have created an idea for it in our Personal Universe and the Law of Balance merely mirrors it back to us in the form of experiences in our life."

Hai San's eyes widened. "Are there exceptions to the Law, Sifu?"

"Exceptions? No, if there are exceptions, how can it be a law? As long as we live, every experience that we have is a mirror of our Personal Universe. So, it follows that if you don't like what you are experiencing, you just have to change your thoughts, feelings and beliefs about yourself and your mirrors will change accordingly."

Hai San's face fell and he grumbled gloomily, "But it's easier said than done, Sifu!"

Sifu Wang chuckled. "But, it's *not* impossible. Not impossible at all," he declared. He got up from the floor and walked to the sideboard to select a small cylinder-like item from a miniature treasure chest. "Come, Hai San, I want you to have an idea of some of the beliefs you hold in your Personal Universe. Take a look at this. This is an 'Isis' pendulum." He fingered the string and allowed it to slide back and forth.

"Oh – what's it for?" Hai San moved forward to peer at the pendulum curiously.

"It is a tool that can be used in many ways," Sifu Wang replied. "You can balance your chakras with it, search for missing items or – " he paused with a mischievous look at his student, "- ask questions of your subconscious self with it." His smile broadened into a grin at the incredulous expression on his student's face.

"What kind of questions can we ask, Sifu?" Hai San was curious.

"Any question which relates to your state of thinking and believing. Let's take your position," Sifu Wang suggested. "You're worried and afraid of not being able to win the school lottery, right?"

Hai San nodded solemnly.

"So, this fear is not a general fear," Sifu Wang analyzed. "It is a fear that is related to your sense of self-worth and your belief about whether or not you deserve to win a prize, or your belief that you can't get something big out of something small or some other beliefs of limitations that you have programmed within your Personal Universe. Whatever they are, you can find them out using the pendulum. When you know what is limiting you, only then can you change your situation for the better. Shall we try it out?"

"Yes, please, Sifu." Hai San eagerly held out his hand.

"Hold the pendulum this way," Sifu Wang instructed. Hai San's heart began to thump. He adjusted his grip on the pendulum. Sifu Wang watched him and nodded his approval. "That's right. Now, ask this question: *Show me the 'yes' direction.*"

Hai San repeated, "Show me the 'yes' direction." The pendulum started swinging and circling. Within a few seconds, it started changing directions and was moving back and forth very strongly.

Sifu Wang nodded. "That's your *'yes'* direction. Now, ask this question: *Show me the 'no' direction.*"

Hai San repeated, "Show me the '*no*' direction." Again, the pendulum started to change direction. It circled for a while and turned this way and that way before swinging sideways very strongly. Both teacher and pupil watched it for a while. Hai San looked up at Sifu Wang with shinning eyes and smiled. "That's my '*no*' direction."

"Yes. Now ask the question: *Do I deserve to win the Perodua?*"

Hai San repeated, *"Do I deserve to win the Perodua?"*

The pendulum started to change directions, swinging this way and that way. Then it circled for a while and finally settled in a *no* direction. Hai San gasped in shock at the moving devise. *It cannot be!* His heart cried out. *His luck surely cannot be that bad!*

"Now, ask the question: *"Do I have low self-worth?"*

Again, Hai San gasped. Sifu was not sparing him any blushes!

Sifu quirked a brow at him. "Go on," he said.

"Do I have low self-worth?" Hai San repeated stoically.

Again, as if the pendulum had a life of its own, it started to change directions. It swung aimlessly for a few seconds and circled a few times before finally moving into a *yes* direction. Hai San looked at the pendulum in dismay. *It cannot be! Please, it cannot be!*

"Okay, that's enough." Sifu Wang broke in kindly and took the pendulum from him.

Hai San slumped, stared down at the floor and blinked rapidly. For a few minutes, he was dumbfounded. A lump the size of a big boulder seemed to have lodged itself in his throat. He felt hurt, pain like never before. He was utterly devastated. *Did he really carry such beliefs within him?* He asked himself desperately. *Did he harbour such liabilities in his Personal Universe?* He raised a hand to wipe across his eyes. *But he had been doing okay so far, hadn't he?*

He tried to gather his scattered thoughts. He knew Sifu was giving him time to collect himself. *It cannot be that bad*, he consoled himself. Finally, with a deep breath, he raised soulful eyes to his teacher.

Sifu Wang looked at him with compassion. 'Nothing has changed, Hai San," he told the boy gently. "Your fears and doubts which we talked about in our last lesson are all related to the baggage that you hold within you. This baggage is your personal story which has given rise to your feelings of low self-worth and deservingness. To enjoy life and achieve whatever you want, you need to recover a good measure of self-worth and deservingness. Otherwise, your personal contempt of Self will block every attempt you make to improve your life and it will always be an uphill journey. Do you understand?"

Hai San nodded, swallowing hard.

"I will teach you to change your programming," Sifu Wang continued. "But before you do so, you need to understand how your issues have come about. To understand, you need to re-visit your past. Some heavy breathing exercises would be in order."

"Breathing exercises?" Hai San asked warily. *Urgh, how much more breathing does he need?*

"Your Breath is your Life," Sifu Wang commented in a light-hearted tone. "Haven't you heard, when God created Man, he breathed life into him? Well, if we want to understand ourselves, we need to breathe life into ourselves. Spiritually speaking, most of us are in a deep coma, Hai San. We need to breathe more deeply to wake ourselves up."

Hai San straightened up. "But I do qi gong everyday, Sifu, I breathe a lot."

Sifu Wang shook his head. "*This* breathing is different."

Just then, there was a knock on the door and Maria peeped in. "Good timing, Maria, come on in," Sifu Wang called out. Maria beamed and came in with a tray of drinks.

"Thanks, Maria."

"A pleasure, Sifu."

As Maria ambled out, Sifu Wang took 2 large mugs from the tray. He handed one to Hai San and said, "Let's take a drink of water first before we start the breathing exercise."

When the last drop was drunk, Sifu Wang said, "We will take about one and a half hours for our breathing exercise. If you need a toilet break, you better take it now."

"Okay. Excuse me, Sifu." Hai San got up to his feet and moved towards the door.

• • •

"Ready?"

"Yes, Sifu."

"Good. What you are going to do now is to breathe deeply in and out rhythmically for one and a half hours. The exercise goes like this – full breath in through the nose, full breath out through the mouth, without any pause. Watch me." Sifu Wang then demonstrated. *Hhm – hahh, hhm – hahh, hhm – hahh, hhm-hahh..*

"You got it?"

"Yes, Sifu," Hai San replied with a little smile. *Oh, this is simple.*

His teacher crooked an eyebrow at him as if reading his thoughts. "Don't pre-judge anything until you have tried it." He pointed to a thin mattress at one corner. "You may lie down on the mattress to be more comfortable."

Hai San spread out the mattress and lay down, waiting for further instructions.

"Are you okay with it?" His teacher looked down at him.

"Yes, Sifu." Hai San managed a slight grin.

"Good. The purpose of this breathing exercise is to move the stored energies within us to rise to the surface for release and integration. As you breathe, you may encounter the stuck energies as aches and pains within your body. That's alright, just allow yourself to feel and continue breathing. There will come a time when you will feel something coming on. Whatever happens, let it happen. If you need to cry, shout, scream, whatever, just allow yourself to do it. Don't suppress it," Sifu Wang instructed. "You can start now."

So, Hai San started his breathing exercise. *Hhm – hahh, hhm – hahh, hhm – hahh, hhm – hahh* and on and on he went. Sifu Wang watched him closely. Fifteen minutes later, Hai San stopped. "No stopping, carry on," Sifu Wang instructed.

"Sifu, I need to catch my breath."

"What's there to catch? You *are* already breathing. Relax and do it rhythmically. Don't over-exert yourself. Go on."

So, Hai San continued with his breathing. *Hhm – hahh, hhm – hahh, hhm – hahh, hhm – hahh....* Another half hour passed. He started feeling aches and cramps in his arms and limbs. He felt cold. He wanted to stop. But Sifu was watching him. So, on and on he went. *Hhm – hahh, hhm – hahh, hhm – hahh, hhm – hahh....*

Suddenly, Hai San felt the raw emotion of anguish flooding over him. A few seconds later, he saw a vision flash across his mind. It was a funeral. "*Ma – – ! Pa – – ! Mei-Mei – – !!*" he cried out as realisation dawned. Hot tears flooded his eyes and began to drip down his face. He was all alone now, an orphan without any sibling. All his regrets began to surface. Sobs wreaked his entire body. Oh, why hadn't he been a better son, a better brother.... why hadn't he had a chance to show them his love.... to say goodbye...why, *why???* His throat felt constricted with a million unanswered questions. It was as if a giant sized boulder had lodged itself there. The hot tears continued to flow in torrents. He wailed out his grief, his remorse. But no matter how he cried, the pain would not go away. He couldn't breathe for his nose had become blocked. His heart felt like it was breaking into a million pieces...

He stopped to blow his nose. Eventually, the boulder at his throat moved, got reduced in size. Another wave of grief...

The boulder moved back into position. Again, he felt his heart breaking into a million pieces. Again, the hot tears flowed uncontrollably. Painful energies were congesting his chest. His hankerchief was all wet now. He lifted up the hem of his shirt and wiped his face with it.

He sat up and took a few deep breaths. He started his rhythm again. *Hhm – hahh, hhm – hahh, hhm – hahh, hhm – hahh* – and the tears continued. He wept some more. And continued his rhythm. *Hhm – hahh, hhm – hahh, hhm –hahh*.... The boulder reduced in size. Then it became smaller – and smaller – and smaller. Finally, his tears dried up. He felt waves of cooling energy washing over him.

A pair of comforting arms wrapped around him. The cooling energy went straight to his heart and was like a balm, soothing it. "Relax," his teacher's voice seem to come from above, "the worst is over." After a while, he was released. "Are you alright now?" His teacher searched his face and smiled. "You can wash up next door," he suggested gently.

Hai San nodded and walked out with his head hung down. When he reached the washroom, he went straight to the mirror. *Yucks, what a sight!* He stared at himself. But, wait – he had a glow on his face which was unusual, despite the reddened nose and puffy eyes. He stared for another minute before he quickly washed his face and toweled it dry. Then he walked back to the Meditation Room.

Sifu Wang smiled at him. "You look much better now. How do you feel?"

"I feel so much lighter now, Sifu, thanks," Hai San said sheepishly.

"Good, good. I want you to practise like this on your own, everyday if possible, for two weeks. Keep a journal by your side and record down whatever you experience, after each session. Just record your feelings, thoughts or any other messages or pictures that you receive. You don't need to analyse them yet. At the end of this period, come and see me again."

Hai San remained quiet.

"What's the matter?" Sifu Wang asked.

"I don't like to do this, Sifu. It's – painful," Hai San said.

"That's because there's resistance and energy blocks in your system. If you don't address it, they'll remain there and forever dominate your life. Do you want your life to be always limited in this way?"

Hai San shook his head and stared at the floor.

Sifu Wang looked at his student with compassion. "It'll get better in time, I promise you." he reassured the boy. "The first few sessions are always more trying. The subsequent ones could be pleasurable, even. Don't be discouraged, okay?"

Hai San looked up at his teacher with a vulnerable expression..

"Don't worry, you'll do great." Sifu Wang said, patting him encouragingly on the shoulder. "If you encounter any problems, call me, okay?"

Hai San nodded.

"At anytime," Sifu Wang added encouragingly.

SEVENTEEN

THE STUDENT UNEARTHED HIS PERSONAL TREASURES

<u>Day One</u> :

"Hhm – hahh, hhm – hahh, hhm – hahh, hhm – hahh...."

What's that? The old man hesitated outside the bedroom door and cocked his ear to one side. He strained his ear for a little while longer and tried to decipher what was happening on the other side of the door. He frowned and shook his head. The sound was reminiscent of days when hormones ran high and couples clamour for privacy in their own rooms. His memories flooded back. He remembered his wife. Oh, sweet Ah Lian. Sweet, sweet Ah Lian who had borne him a son and three daughters, and worked alongside him through the difficult years.

"Hhm – hahh, hhm – hahh, hhm – hahh, hhm – hahh... The rhythm continued. "Hhm – hahh, hhm – hahh, hhm – hahh, hhm – hahh...

The old man sighed. But, she had gone away too early, his heart whispered, *way too early*. He shook his head in regret and ambled towards the living room.

An hour later, he switched off the television. He glanced at the clock. Seven – it's time for dinner. *I wonder if Boy is ready for food.* He ambled towards his grandson's bedroom. Hhm – hahh, hhm – hahh, hhm – hahh... It was still ongoing. Suddenly, he heard muffled sounds of crying. He stopped in his track and cocked his ear once again. Yes, his grandson was crying. He was sure of it. But *why*? What had Sifu Wang been teaching him? He lifted his hand to rap on the door but dropped it on second thoughts. He would wait for Boy to explain. He ambled again to the living room and searched for his favourite magazine to read.

Meanwhile, alone in his room, Hai San was sobbing out the last vestige of his pain and misery. He blew his nose a couple of times with tissues and took a few slow breaths to regain control of himself. He didn't know why he had so much sadness in him. This was his second breathing exercise and he didn't know if he wanted to continue. All he had experienced was pain and more pain. He had learnt to recognise the pain by now. It was a low frequency energy that seemed 'loaded'. At times, however, he felt that it contained some anger as well, particularly when it shot up into his mouth cavity and shook the roots of his pre-molar. He shuddered as he recalled the intensity of that angry energy. His tears had come in full force then. He didn't even know why he felt it was an angry energy. He just intuited it that way.

He leafed slowly through the pages of his home made journal and wondered achingly what he should write about. Finally he scrawled the word "Pain" across the page. Beneath the word, he added in bullet points – 1) heavy, loaded energy 2) grief 3) anger 4) attack on teeth and gums. He hadn't received any message or vision. Sifu might be disappointed with him. But he would not care anymore. The whole exercise was too painful. He wanted *out*. He would tell Sifu that.

He walked out of his room to the bathroom at the back of the house to wash his face. He hoped his Grandpa would not notice his puffy eyes and reddened nose. The last thing he wanted was an inquisition especially if it involved his personal pain. He had no answers for his grandfather. He had none even for himself.

Hai San walked into the living room. The old man looked up surreptitiously from his magazine and cleared his throat. Hai San looked at his grandfather and smiled sheepishly.

'Dinner time, Grandpa. I'll go and collect the food," he said to his grandfather in a nasal voice. Their dinner was catered by a neighbour a few doors away since neither Hai San nor his grandfather were great at cooking. It was hardly worth the trouble anyway to do the marketing and organise a kitchen just to cook for two persons.

His grandfather observed his puffy eyes and put down his magazine. "I'll get it. I need to stretch my legs," he said.

"Thanks, Grandpa. I'll set the table."

Ten minutes later, they were seated at their dining table with an array of dishes set before them. Hai San smilingly surveyed the food and mentally gave his thanks to the universe for this banquet and to all the people responsible for bringing it to his table. Then he dipped his spoon into his favourite curry dish and proceeded to mix the sauce with his rice. He took in a few mouthfuls and declared happily, "'Aunt Maggie excels herself every time with her vegetable curry."

"Hmm," his grandfather grunted.

Hai San looked up at his grandfather and smiled. His Grandpa must like the curry a lot to not want to make conversation. Either that or it's too fiery. Yeah, that must be it. He could feel steam coming out of his own ears and temple as he savoured the potent spices.

When they had finished their meal, Hai San stood up to gather the plates to wash. But his grandfather waved for him to sit down again. "Leave the plates, Boy. You can wash them afterwards," the old man instructed. Hai San sat down abruptly. *What does Grandpa want now?* he wondered.

The old man drew out a cheroot from its casing, fiddled with it and put it between his lips to light it. Then he drew in a few puffs. Hai San waited with bated breaths. When the silence seemed to go on forever, the old man began, "Your lessons with Sifu Wang – do you like what you've learnt so far?"

"Yes, Grandpa."

"Good. Do you find them – useful?"

"Yes, Grandpa."

"Great. Tell me what you have learnt."

"Er– " Hai San searched his mind for a tactful answer. He could not refuse to answer to his grandfather. But at the same time, he did not want to reveal too much of what he had learnt lest Sifu thought he had leaked out the Secrets. "Er – Grandpa – as you know it's about the Secrets. The Secrets involves understanding who we are, where our power comes from, how to deal with challenging situations given that We Are That We Are and well – er – how to be a Super Being. Yes, that's it – *How to Be a Super-Duper Being*. That's what the Secrets is about."

"Hmm." His grandfather studied him curiously. "And is making funny noises in your room part of the Secrets?"

Hai San stiffened. He stared at his grandfather in disbelief. Having waited in suspense for the last couple of minutes, he had not suspected that his grandfather had such a perception. He opened his mouth to answer but closed it again. Then he turned away, his shoulders slumped and slowly began to shake. His grandfather looked at him as if he had gone mad.

"Oh, Grandpa!" Hai San cried out, holding his stomach and trying to contain his laughter. "It's only a breathing exercise."

"What kind of breathing exercise?" the old man persisted.

"Just breathing in and out. Sifu said it will bring out the energies of the past to the surface so that we can release them," Hai San replied.

His grandfather studied him for a few seconds and then asked, "Suppose you show me?"

"Oh, alright," Hai San said, trying to maintain his composure. He straightened up, cleared his throat a bit and took a deep breath through his nose – "hhm" – and blew out through his mouth – "hahh". Then he looked at his grandfather and repeated, "hhm – hahh, hhm – hahh, hhm – hahh, hhm – hahh…"

"That's enough. I don't want your curry breath all over me," the old man said gruffly.

Hai San stole a look at his grandfather, certain that he had been censured. But the old man was grinning away. Relieved, Hai San grinned back. His grandfather was okay with the breathing exercise.

"Grandpa, Sifu asked me to practise daily for two weeks."

"Well, he must have good reason to ask you to do that."

"But I'm thinking of opting out, Grandpa."

"Why? It's not like you to opt out of anything." The old man looked askance at his grandson.

"It takes a lot of my time, Grandpa. And it's a painful exercise," Hai San made his excuses.

"Why don't you talk it over with Sifu? Maybe he can modify it for you, make it less painful?"

"I don't think so, Grandpa. I've already spoken with Sifu. He said if I don't do it, the past will always come in to interfere with my life."

"Well, then," his grandfather said shortly. "You know what to do."

• • •

Hai San went to bed that night with a lot of misgivings. He wanted *out* but his grandfather had expected him to do otherwise. His grandfather had the highest respect for Sifu and despite feeling initially curious, perhaps even suspicious about the 'funny noises', he had very quickly quashed his own doubts and understood the purpose. His grandfather therefore could not be an ally if he had to tell Sifu that he was opting out. So, what excuse could he give Sifu without appearing weak-kneed and gutless? Hai San mulled over his options. Could he say he had a lot of school work or that his examinations were approaching or that he had school projects to participate in? No, that would not be possible. That would only be temporary at best ....Or what about....? He yawned and closed his eyes wearily.

Suddenly his grandfather appeared before him. "You know what to do, don't you? You want to ride in a Mercedes or take a bus all your life?" his grandfather demanded.

"Oh, Grandpa – " Hai San tried to protest.

"Not another word from you. Do you hear?"

Hai San hung down his head and sniffed. *Who doesn't want to ride in a Mercedes?* It's unfair of Grandpa to say it in this way. Grandpa had not experienced the emotional pain nor the stiffening of his limbs as if it had been in deep freeze. It was unfair, really unfair...

He was practising the breathing exercise again. His friend, Ken Chye strolled in and stopped short at his feet, shaking his head in feigned sympathy. "Tut, tut, so much difficulty just to win a Perodua," his friend taunted, "you might as well give up and let me win."

"No! No – !" Hai San cried out. "Please go away – "

"Hhm – hahh, hhm – hahh, hhm – hahh," he was still doing the breathing exercise. ....Or was he? There was no longer any stiffness in his arms and limbs. He felt a certain stillness about the atmosphere. Something had changed. It was as if the energy around him had shifted. His body had become very relaxed. A low humming sound was coming from within him. It started as a vibration from his solar plexus and it was moving up and up towards his throat. Suddenly, he realised it was his own voice reverberating from within and it was saying ever so slowly, "Hai... Sa..an.. don't... keep... your...old energy.....let... go...o..o"

"What?" Hai San pulled himself up from his bed and peered blinkingly into the semi-darkness. His heart was thumping very fast. But every thing in the room appeared normal. There was the usual clickety sound of his ceiling fan and the soft glow of his bedside lamp casting shadows on the wall and floor. He had not imagined hearing the message, had he? The voice within had sounded like his own voice and had advised him to let go off his old energy. That meant he should continue with his breathing exercise. Hai San took a few deep breaths and tried to recall what he had just experienced. So – ok – the early part of it with his Grandpa and Ken Chye was a dream. Perhaps, it came from his fears and uncertainties. But the last message was very real. He was sure of it. It had been unlike the other two and the voice had been his, coming from inside of him. He had felt himself partially awake when the vibrations came on. *Wow!* His heart took a leap. He had had a connection with his Inner Self, *hadn't he?*

Day Two:

Hai San walked into the living room and smiled at his grandfather. It was four in the afternoon. He had already completed his school work and had some free time to spare before he began his breathing exercise.

"Grandpa, you don't mind if I watch *Doraemon* for a while?" he asked, walking over to the television set.

The old man looked up from his newspapers and smiled at his grandson. "As long as you've completed your school work, you can go ahead with whatever you want to do."

"Thanks, Grandpa, but will it disturb your reading?"

"No, no, you just go ahead, Boy."

Hai San happily switched on his favourite programme and settled down on a footstool a few feet away from his grandfather. Ten minutes into the programme, he was already chuckling away at the antics of his favourite characters and slamming his palms against his thighs when the humour got away from him.

That funny, huh? The old man glanced sideways at the boy and then peered at the television before turning back to his papers again. Twenty minutes later, the episode ended.

"Best TV programme!" Hai San declared to no one in particular and cheerfully got up to switch off the television. He walked back to his seat, paused and looked at his grandfather before making his announcement, "I'm going to do my breathing exercise now, Grandpa. I don't want to be disturbed."

"Hmm," the old man grunted without looking up. "I won't disturb you unless there's a fire."

Hai San burst out laughing and went into the kitchen to get himself a big mug of water which he proceeded to gulp down. Then he went to his bedroom and prepared for his exercise. A few minutes later, the sound of hhm – hahh, hhm – hahh, hhm – hahh…could be heard in the room. This time round, however, the old man did not bother to listen at the door. He remained in his favourite armchair in the living room, reading his papers and seemed oblivious to any goings-on in his grandson's room.

Hai San felt the low frequency energy surfacing in his body. But the stiffness in his limbs had been less intense now. He had learnt how to pace his breathing more rhythmically and as a result, was able to relax more.

Three quarters way into the exercise, he heard a voice inside him saying rather regretfully, "Grandpa, I have done wrong." *Oh my gosh, what's that? The voice had sounded – like – Doraemon's!* He was stunned. He stopped his rhythm. *How could it be? Have I gone mad or what?* he asked himself. Never in a million years could he have guessed that this would happen. Then he remembered what his teacher had said. Don't analyse – just record everything down. So he continued his breathing. Hhm – hahh, hhm – hahh, hhm – hahh….

Ten minutes later, a few pictures flashed in succession through his mind. They showed a young man slowly edging his way from among the roof tops of some old fashioned buildings. It was dark, almost midnight. The waters were rising and he appeared to be trying to escape from a flood. Everywhere was quiet. Then came the sound of moaning from below, a low anguished kind of sound. That of a woman in pain. The young man stopped short and cocked his ear to listen. The sound seemed to come from the very house below his feet. He parted a few roof tiles and took a peep inside. He was shocked. A young woman was writhing in pain. A very pregnant young woman indeed with the flood waters almost half way up to her makeshift bed. The youth was undecided. Should he go in and help the woman? But what could he do? Just then, he felt raindrops coming down fast and furious. The rain had started again. As if propelled by some urgent need, the youth quickly closed back the roof tiles and crept along the rooftops. Darkness surrounded him once again. *Oh, no – it can't be me!* Hai San wailed in agony. *I'm not like that! I wouldn't deliberately let a woman die!* Tears ran down his cheeks. He had such a lump in his throat and his chest was congested with pain. He clutched his pillow to his chest and sobbed uncontrollably. *I'm not like that! Not like that – not like that-* he protested. But the evidence was clear enough....

"Grandpa, I have done wrong." His inner voice had said, never mind that it sounded like Doraemon.

Hai San sobbed into his pillow. He felt the lump in his throat and tried to breathe deeply in and out to clear it. Finally, it cleared and with it, his tears also dried up. Then, he sat up in his bed and sadly recalled the visions. He had been *oh, so utterly despicable. Selfish. Thinking only of himself.* Some fresh tears came up and he lifted a hand to wipe them away. He took a few deep calming breaths. It had been him, hadn't it? He was that young man! He took a few more deep breaths. Sifu had said not to analyse. Wearily, he opened his home-made journal and wrote down what Doraemon had said. Then he briefly described the visions that had flashed through his mind like excerpts from a mini-series.

Day Three:

"Grandpa, I've borrowed a video tape on Superman. Would you like to watch?" Hai San asked his grandfather.

"Superman? The one with the body stockings and red cape who can fly through the air?"

"Yeah – that's the one." Hai San grinned widely at his grandfather's description.

"I'm game. Put it on, boy," his grandfather said and went over to settle down in his favourite armchair before the TV.

They watched the movie in rapt attention with Hai San making brief translations and commentaries along the way for his grandfather. Three quarters way through, while Superman was trying to rescue some people from a burning building, Hai San heard an unmistakable snore beside him. He stole a sideway glance and smiled. His grandfather was in dreamland as usual, at 3.00 every afternoon. He turned down the volume and continued to watch until the end where Superman triumphed once again by saving the city from unscrupulous crooks. Then he switched it off and left his grandfather to his afternoon snooze while he began his third day of breathing practice.

Hhm – hahh, hhm – hahh, hhm – hahh, hhm – hahh...Hai San had been practicing for three quarters of an hour and nothing happened except aching bones and stiff limbs. God, it was painful. This low level energy inside him. He felt like giving it up. But he thought of his earlier message, "Hai Sa-an...don't keep your energy..let go...let go.."

He continued his rhythm. Hhm – hahh, hhm – hahh, hhm – hahh, hhm – hahh...he went on for another fifteen minutes. Suddenly, a couple of motion pictures flashed before his eyes. Wait a minute – who was this young man? And the woman with the baby? Hai San felt anguish whelming up within him. He felt all wrong and disorientated. Oh dear, she was crying, holding on to him and begging him to stay. The baby was squalling away but both adults were not taking any notice. Suddenly, the young man pulled away, despair seen in the slouch of his shoulders. He seemed adamant to go. He had to leave. He did not love the woman. It was an arranged marriage...

Hhm – hahh, hhm – hahh, hhm – hahh, hhm – hahh...The next scene saw the young man crossing a river in an old ferry with scores of other people, a satchel containing his meagre belongings slung on his shoulders. He looked ahead to the horizon, tensed and anxious. Hai San felt his limbs stiffen further. Raw pain caught at his throat. Hhm – hahh, hhm – hahh, hhm – hahh....The tears came slowly, then it became a flood. His pillow was all wet.

Another picture appeared. He was seen with hundreds of others, all wearing nothing but tattered singlets and cotton underpants, doggedly hacking at rocks with chisels and pickles. Suddenly, there was a shout and what appeared like an avalanche of sand, stones and rocks came hurtling down. Confusion reigned. There were cries of panic from everywhere. Then all of a sudden, the sky seemed to drop down with a big whooping sound. Darkness reigned. And an eerie kind of silence...

Hai San sobbed his hearts out. He sobbed for the lack of love and the anger, the guilt and the unfulfilled dreams of the young man who had left his matrimonial home to seek his fortune and died while on the job. He sobbed until the pain at his throat cleared and he could breathe normally again. Then wearily, he took out his home-made journal and began to write.

Oh, why couldn't he have good stories to write about? The tears fell once again and he brushed it aside. It's all sob, sob stories. He wasn't even given a chance to live and make a fresh start...

• • •

Dinner was an uneventful affair. If his grandfather had noticed his puffy eyes, he pretended otherwise. After that, Hai San washed up, did his homework and went to bed.

Right in the middle of the night, a storm broke out. Part of the hillslopes broke away and rocks, stones and mud slid down rapidly into the houses at the foot. Hai San got up with a start. His home had been partially buried. He tried to open his door but it was stuck, glued by mud and debris. He panicked and started to shout for help. Suddenly, Superman appeared at his window and shook his head, "It's no use. I can't help bad characters like you. You left a wife and baby to fend for themselves." He pointed an accusing finger at Hai San. "You! You are irresponsible – bad – not worthy of rescue." "Oh, help me, please," Hai San cried out. "I know I've done wrong. I'll – I'll put things right. I'll do anything. *Help me!*"

Superman laughed aloud in disbelief.

"You can't leave me here!" Hai San cried out in panic.

"Watch me." Superman swirled around with his cape, flexed his broad shoulders and flew out of the window.

"NO..O…O..O..!!!"

Hai San sat up abruptly in his bed, breathing loudly. He stared at his door, then at the window and the rest of his room. Everything appeared normal. So, it was just a dream. He sighed in relief. A bad dream. But how long is this going to continue? Sifu had said to practise for two weeks. This was just the third day and already he felt like he had been in a roller coaster a number of times. He was not going to be able to sleep after this. It was too claustrophobic, too traumatic, too much of everything wrong. With resignation, he took out his home-made journal and in the dimmed light of his bed lamp, recorded the contents of his dream.

Day Nine:

Hai San clutched the pillow to his chest and sobbed in anguish.

No, it couldn't be! It couldn't be! He was not this woman. She had no morals. He couldn't be her! No, no! A part of him denied it. But *yes – yes*, it's true, another part was telling him. It was all true – and he was the woman who had not only allowed herself to be touched all over but had been an active participant. She was the aggressor – had seemed to enjoy it – and there had been different partners...

Hai San shuddered as he recalled the shameless visions and wept. NO...O...O..! *How could he face Sifu ever again?* He sniffed into his pillow. The visions that had flashed through his mind could not have come from thin air. He knew that. They were stored memories of his past and they had come up to the surface for resolution. But how was he going to resolve them? No way was he going to tell Sifu what he had seen. *No way!* That was his private story. He bowed his head. His shoulders slumped in utter defeat.

He felt *bad* and *worthless*. If his friends and relatives were to know, they would surely look on him as an outcast. And where would he be? He took in a few deep breaths. He needed to decide what to do next. What should he tell Sifu? Should he fabricate something? *No, I really couldn't lie to Sifu.* So, how about packaging the stories a bit so he wouldn't look too bad? *No, that's not right, either.*

All of the visions he had were negative no matter how he was going to package it unless he did a total fabrication. But he couldn't lie to Sifu. And Sifu would know, anyway. A bad past is bad enough, should it be compounded with a bad present as well? *Oh, what a confusion this is!* Well, maybe he would play a waiting game...delay reporting to Sifu... so after a time, maybe Sifu would not be so insistent on wanting to know everything. Maybe he would tell a bit and leave the rest for Sifu to guess?

A telephone shrilled in the background.

Yes, that would be it. I'll go see Sifu after a lapse of...perhaps three weeks. I'll plead busyness with school work...

The old man knocked on his grandson's bedroom door. "Boy, your phone. Sifu on the line."

Hai San's heart gave a lurch. Deadline over! Heart pounding, he dragged himself off his bed to open his door and reluctantly walked out to the hallway.

"Hello, Sifu! Hai San here," he greeted his teacher in a nasal voice.

"Hello, Hai San! How're you doing?" Sifu sounded too cheerful.

"Er…er..ok, I guess."

There was a chuckle at the end of the line. "Enjoyed yourself with the breathing exercises, didn't you?"

Oh, Sifu must know! Hai San took a gulp of fresh air. *He's making fun of me!*

"Er, Sifu, as a matter of fact, I…I haven't done much…my school work..you know?"

There was a pause at the other end of the line. "Never mind, Hai San, complete at least seven breathing sessions and we'll discuss it next Saturday. Now, in the meantime, I want you to fix an appointment for me with Madame Tang this Saturday. You don't have to be present if you're busy."

"Oh – oh alright, Sifu." Damn, he was caught in his own trap! Now, he couldn't be present when Sifu discussed with Madam Tang the next stage of healing. "Would 10.00am be alright?"

"Make it around 9.00am."

"Ok, then. I'll get back to you, Sifu."

"That would be great. Thanks, Hai San."

"You're welcome, Sifu!" Hai San replied. He replaced the receiver and turned to slump onto a nearby sofa.

"Why, what's wrong, boy?" His grandfather appeared in the hallway.

"Nothing, Grandpa, just that – that – life is getting too complicated, that's all." Hai San threw an arm over his face and slumped down further onto the sofa.

The old man raised a brow at this pronouncement. *What is this? Life is supposed to get smoother and easier with the Secrets, isn't it? What complication is his grandson talking about?* He shook his head at this new riddle.

● ● ●

EIGHTEEN

THE TEACHER MET WITH RESISTANCE

'**D**ING – DONG.'
Damn, damn, damn. Who could it be so early in the morning? Ken Chye closed his eyes sleepily before he slowly opened them again. Taking a deep breath, he reluctantly got up from the sofa and walked towards the front door, leaving the morning papers to fall untidily into a heap on the floor. He stretched himself along the way and arched his neck dramatically to give justice to his third yawn since getting up. *Wah..uh..ah*

He opened the door with a flourish and stopped abruptly. "Oh!" he gulped. "Oh, Sifu, come on in."

"Good morning, Ken Chye!" Sifu Wang smiled broadly and stepped in. "I hope I haven't woken you up from sleep?"

"No, no. I was already up." Ken Chye hastily denied. "And er, good morning to you, too, Sifu! Won't you take a seat? I'll inform my Mother you're here." He bent down to quickly pick up the papers.

"Sure. Take your time. I'm early."

Ken Chye hurried towards the kitchen. "Mum," he said in a loud whisper. "Sifu is here," he mouthed, pointing to the living room.

Madam Tang's eyes widened. She put up a hand to smoothen her hair. "So early?" she mouthed back.

Ken Chye shrugged and raised his eyes heavenwards.

Madam Tang quickly dried her hands and untied her apron. "I'm not ready yet," she muttered, looking down at her housecoat. She took a deep breath and striving for normalcy, walked towards the living room.

"Good morning, Sifu." She smiled hesitantly at her healer. "You're early," she studiously pointed out.

"Good morning, Madam." Sifu Wang stood up to greet her cheerfully. "I must apologise for that. I see the fine weather today…" he tailed off and gestured smilingly towards the open window. "And I couldn't resist the idea of taking a drive to the coast for some seafood noodles. Join me?"

"Oh." Madam Tang was flustered. "Oh, thank you – this is a surprise."

"Good. We all need to be surprised from time to time, don't we?" Sifu Wang replied, grinning cheekily.

"Er, I supposed so. But I'm not dressed. Could you give me ten minutes?"

"Sure."

"Would you like some coffee while you wait?"

"No, thanks. I'm alright. I'll just have a look at the news." Sifu Wang indicated the papers in his hands.

"Ok. I'll try to be quick." Madam Tang replied.

"Take your time." Sifu Wang said.

• • •

The seafood noodles proved to be delicious and the company, riveting. Madam Tang had not thought Sifu Wang could be so well traveled and knowledgeable. After a second helping and a second cup of coffee, she sat back in her chair and smiled lazily. "This is great. I could get used to this – fresh air, blue sky and the tastiest noodles I've ever eaten. Now, I don't feel like going back home to do housework," she admitted.

Sifu Wang chuckled. "Housekeeping is noble work," he commented.

"Is it?" Madam Tang raised an eyebrow in disbelief.

"Yes," Sifu Wang replied with a gleam in his eyes. "Imagine a house that is topsy-turvy, where everything is not in its place. Or one that is covered with dust. They are all indications of confusion and neglect," Sifu Wang said. Madam Tang's eyes rounded.

"Our house is an extension of Our Self", Sifu Wang continued with a smile. "At the same time, it is also within Us, within Our Personal

Universe, if you like. If it is not in order, we will have Problems in our life."

"Really, how?" Madam Tang was curious.

"Everything in life exists in a *holographic* pattern, Madam. That means everything we see in our Outer World is also within Us, within Our Personal Universe, within each tiny cell, within our DNA. Yet at the same time, that entire world in the tiny cell, in the DNA, is also a part of the bigger external world. Can you imagine the beauty of this?" Sifu Wang's eyes twinkled with delight

"Uh – huh." Madam Tang frowned and bit her lip, trying to understand such Wisdom that is beyond her.

Sifu Wang smiled and leaned forward to ask, "If your house in your Outer World is not in order, what does that say for your house in your Inner World?"

Madam Tang felt a jolt ran through her. She thought of her home previously and Sifu's comments about it. To her dismay, she felt warmth flooding up her face.

"I suppose – it will not be in order," she replied reluctantly.

"Exactly!" Sifu beamed with delight. "Because they're one and the same. So, what does that tell you about the condition or the health of your body?"

"They – they're sick?" she asked uncertainly.

"Let's say, your body won't be functioning at par and that's because everything in life also exists as *mirrors* of each other. The mess and the disorganized state of the house will cause everything in its surroundings to – well – mimic back in kind."

Madam Tang hastily raised her coffee cup to her lips. Her face flushed as she silently considered the burning question: *Could the state of her house have caused her the dis-ease?*

"It takes more than a neglected house to cause cancer." Sifu Wang said, seeming to read her mind. "Cancer is an aggressive dis-ease. When a person gets it, it's a MAJOR WAKE UP CALL."

"Wake – wake up call to what?" Madam Tang struggled to get the words out, fear tightening up her tongue.

Sifu Wang leaned back in his chair and surveyed her calmly before replying, "Some issues that are seeking resolution, my dear. It may be an aspect or aspects of Our Self that are seeking release from their perceived suffering. Or it may be a milestone indicator that the Soul devises for the Human Self to decide whether it wants to continue with its current course or end it."

Madam Tang visibly shuddered. Talks of souls and the intangible and unseen almost always unnerve her.

"You know," Sifu Wang said. "You're one of the most responsive healees I've ever encountered. Hardly two months and you're almost back to normal. I've had some healees who take more than six months to show results."

Almost? Madam Tang paled, panic rising within her. "Whatever do you mean, Sifu? I don't have any more pain."

"Don't be alarmed, Madam. You are alright now and will be for some time. I've made sure of that. But, in the long term, you might want to consider a TOTAL HEALING. A total healing involves healing your personal issues."

"What personal issues?" Madam Tang sniffed.

Sifu Wang smiled. "Only you know what personal issues you have, Madam."

"I don't have any." Madam Tang retorted tartly.

Sifu Wang smiled and shook his head. "Everybody has personal issues."

"Do you?" Madam Tang challenged Sifu.

"Sure, but nothing I cannot handle." Sifu Wang replied smoothly.

Madam Tang sniffed.

"It's imperative, my dear that you learn to do self-healing," Sifu Wang said smilingly. "The blockage in your liver may have disappeared. But their energy hasn't. Right now, my guess is they're circulating within your energy field. One day they're going to settle somewhere and cause a blockage again *if* you don't do anything to resolve them now."

"You're trying to frighten me, aren't you, Sifu?" Madam Tang eyed Sifu Wang suspiciously, while hunching her shoulders defensively.

"On the contrary I want to open your eyes to what you're not seeing, my dear. Energy by nature cannot simply disappear of its own accord. It has to be resolved through self-acceptance and forgiveness. Learning and practicing how to breathe helps tremendously in the process."

Madam Tang frowned and placed a hand at her throat in partial distress.

"I don't think I want to hear this anymore, Sifu. Can't you give me a few more healing sessions?"

Sifu wang leaned back in his chair and regarded her solemnly. "I have done whatever I can. The next stage of healing depends on you."

"Me? Why does it have to be *me*?" Madam Tang demanded.

"Because it's your Energy and your Baggage, that's causing your problem," Sifu Wang answered calmly. "The "You" that you are in the past are seeking to be released from their unhappy stories. And It or They are causing blocks in your etheric and physical energy field."

Madam Tang shook her head vehemently to reject any further clarification from Sifu. She lifted up her hands to cover her ears.

Sifu Wang looked on with compassion and kept quiet.

Madam Tang breathed heavily in agitation. Finally, pale faced, she asked in a trembling voice, "So, what do I have to do, Sifu?"

"Nothing complex, my dear. Just give yourself some time everyday for healing. How you heal is through your BREATH. Breathe deeply in and out, into your belly, four to five sessions a day, each time for fifteen to twenty minutes."

"Is that all?" Madam Tang asked sharply, disbelief colouring her voice.

"That's the gist of it. I would like to guide you through the sessions, though."

She sniffed. "If it's as simple as that, why isn't everyone doing it? For that matter, why isn't it taught in the hospitals?"

"Very few are aware of how healing works, Madam. For that matter, why wouldn't *you* want to do it?" Sifu Wang countered evenly.

Madam Tang's expression changed. Pouting, she gathered up her purse and made as if to stand up and leave.

"I'm sorry. I didn't mean to upset you." Sifu Wang said quietly, standing up to stop her. "Please – sit down."

Madam Tang remained standing for a while but she finally sank back into her seat. She felt her eyes watered and blinked rapidly. Suddenly, it was as if her whole world was crashing in on her once again. She was back to square one. *Oh, why? Why does this have to happen to her?* She wanted to scream out.

Sifu Wang looked at her in deep sympathy. He said in a patient voice, "You want to be healed, don't you?"

Madam Tang stared stonily ahead into the horizon.

Sifu Wang continued gently, "If I could heal you all the way, my dear, I would. But it's not possible. Nobody outside of Your Self can be your healer. Healing always has to be a personal choice and you always need to take the Lead Role yourself. This is because the energy causing the Dis-ease is yours and nobody elses. Therefore only *you* can resolve it. Do you understand?"

He smiled encouragingly at her. But Madam Tang had withdrawn into her shell. He had expected resistance and Resistance was sitting right in front of him.

He leaned back in his chair and felt her aloneness, her panic and her fear. Her energies were in havoc. He could not do much for the moment except to allow her to be. Hopefully, she would feel the strength, the stability and the balance of his energy and come round. Some people were just not opened to new and simple ways of doing things. They had been too used to struggling and striving to ever want to believe in Miracles. And some preferred the surgeon's knife, thinking that it would solve everything. He feel frustrated at times like this. The solution is always so simple. But few would listen.

He called for the bill and spoke to the proprietor for a few minutes. "Come, Madam, let us go."

On the drive back, both were silent. She was busy with her own misery and he was understanding enough to leave her alone. When the car came to a halt outside her home, he opened the car door for her and said gently, "Thank you for your company, my dear. You will think about what I've said, won't you?"

She didn't answer except to mutter a quick "Thanks for the breakfast, Sifu" before fleeing inside.

• • •

Back in her own room, she clutched her pillow to her chest and sobbed quietly. *ALMOST HEALED*...Sifu had said. *Oh, why? Why does this have to happen to her? Why, on top of a cruel Mother-in-law – and being a widow at a relatively young age, why does she have to have this – this affliction, this dis-ease, of all things?*

Why can't she be like her friends – Mary, Betty or Angela? Why can't she have perfect lives like them – people to love them, people to take care of them… and….no bills… no money problem… no disease…. to worry about? Why is God so unfair??? She sobbed pitifully into her pillow.

Meanwhile, outside, the beautiful blue sky that had adorned the early morning hours was already turning dark. Grey clouds moved swiftly as if to prepare for a thunderstorm. Shutters banged against window frames as South Westerly winds challenged their very existence.

"Mum? Mum! It's going to rain!" Ken Chye shouted from the hallway. When there was no answer from the room, he dashed out with the laundry basket to hastily clear the laundry line.

Very soon, rain drops were heard furiously beating on the roof and ground outside. Madam Tang, however, was oblivious to her surroundings. She was too immersed in her own misery to care.

Oh, why did Sifu Wang mislead her? Why did he say she could be healed when he did not want to heal her completely? And why tell her to breathe a ridiculous number of times a day? She beat furiously at her pillow as her tears ran hot and fast. She sobbed until she could hardly breathe. Finally, when she was spent, she curled into a ball at the foot of her bed and slept the sleep of the tortured.

NINETEEN

THE STUDENT LEARNT ABOUT ASPECTS AND MIRRORS

Thursday came. By then, Hai San had done another three sessions of breathing. It was difficult. Each session appeared to be more challenging than the last. Now, he had been a workaholic scientist, a corrupt ruler, a nineteenth century spy, a crazy dominican nun, a failure of a Red Indian chief, a scheming eunuch, an irresponsible husband and father, a selfish man... and oh, the unmentionable quote unquote... *How was he ever going to face Sifu with all these revelations! How could he hold up his head with dignity now?*

Hai San worried day and night. But Sifu Wang was not going to let him get away so easily. Sifu had called in the afternoon to confirm a lesson for Saturday morning which was not a norm. It was usually he, Hai San, who called up Sifu to confirm. Now it was the other way round. There was no evading Sifu....

• • •

Hai San reluctantly brought his bicycle to a stop at his favourite parking place under a mango tree.

A scream broke out from above. He looked up tiredly. *Now what?* Arms and legs appeared to be tangling with branches.

"Hey, you! Get your thing away from my tree," cried the voice from above.

Ah, a hooligan. Hai San was not going to be bothered. He had better things to do. He parked his bicycle at his usual spot, all the while conscious of the deliberate rustling of leaves and branches overhead.

A cry like the sound of a banshee pierced through the air. "Uuuuuuuueeeewaaauuuuu--! – Go away !"

"No – no – no, you stup!" A loud thud sounded. The hooligan had obviously landed. Hai San walked towards the porch regardless.

'Hey – hey!" *How rude.* He had no time for childish hysterics. As far as he was concerned, Sifu had never made any objections as to where he parked his bicycle. An apparition of Arms and Legs continued to remonstrate with him. Just as he was about to ring the doorbell, he felt a tug at his sleeve. He took a deep breath and turned exasperatedly towards Arms and Legs. For an instant, he was taken aback. Standing before him was the scrawniest girl he had ever seen.

"Did you hear what I said!" Arms and Legs shrilled and stamped her foot in frustration. "Get – your – 'cycle off *my* place."

"*Your place?*" Hai San was indignant. "Little Girl, I've got permission from Sifu!" he retorted.

The door opened in a flurry. Maria stood, frowning at the two younger people. "What's all this noise? Lily Tharmalingam, it's time for your dancing lessons. Come on in, Hai San." She smiled her welcome.

Arms and Legs turned and pulled her tongue out at Hai San. He ignored the childish gesture and instead greeted Maria with a grateful smile.

Arms and Legs squeezed her way through the doorway in between Hai San and Maria and held her arms towards Sifu Wang who had just appeared from the back.

'Ah Gong, somebody bullied me just now," she said tearfully as she clung to the older man.

What..! Hai San was aghast at the accusation. He opened his mouth to deny. But Sifu was looking straight at him over the skinny frame with a gleam in his eyes. Oh-oh.

"Poppet, who dared to bully you?" Sifu Wang held Arms and Legs tenderly and smoothened her wild scraggly hair. "I'm sure they'd learn to regret it," he said with some humour.

"But, I was, Ah Gong." Brown eyes sniffed for effect and darted an accusing look at Hai San.

Hai San stiffened indignantly.

"Mmm." Her grandfather chuckled and rubbed her back affectionately. 'Now, why don't you go clean up? I'll drive you to Aunty Belle's."

Arms and Legs raised her head and peeped at her grandfather impishly. "Okay," she said. "Okay, Ah Gong!" she repeated and gave him a hug before she scooted off.

Sifu Wang looked on indulgently and then smiled at Hai San. "Hi, Hai San, give me ten minutes, won't you? I'll see you in the Meditation Room."

"Ok, Sifu," he smiled back at his teacher.

• • •

"I'm sorry about all that, Hai San." Sifu Wang said on entering the Meditation Room. "And thanks for your patience. My grand daughter, Lily, is not at her best at the moment. Her mother, that is, my daughter, has just given birth to twins and with all the attention levied on the two new born, she is feeling very much left out. I guess she wants to hit out at somebody. But don't worry, she'll get out of her tantrum in no time."

"Oh, I see." Hai San managed a smile.

Sifu Wang smiled at Hai San. "Please excuse her."

He topped up Hai San's glass with some fruit juice and filled one for himself. He sipped and leaned back on some cushions before he continued with wry amusement, "Nonetheless, things do not happen without cause, Hai San. You might want to consider that she is holding a Mirror for you."

"A Mirror?" *What mirror?*

"Do you remember what I taught you, Hai San, that what you hold in your Personal Universe will be reflected back to you as experiences in daily life? What do you think happened just now?"

Hai San frowned. He was unfairly accused, alright. And the little girl, Lily, had been antagonistic right from the time he got down from his bicycle. *Unreasonably* so. But could he tell Sifu that?

"Well, er, Sifu..." Hai San hesitated.

"It's ok, Hai San, you can be forthright with me."

"Well, I..er.. think …I was unfairly accused. I don't know your grand daughter and she doesn't know me and there's no reason for her behaviour. She didn't want me to park my bicycle at any place and in fact, she wanted to chase me out!" Hai San said, the last sentence in an outraged voice.

Sifu Wang chuckled. "Well, well – Hai San – things are becoming very interesting for you now," he commented.

Hai San stiffened, his shoulders ramrod straight, and glowered. *Interesting? Hah, Sifu must be jesting!*

"It appears," Sifu Wang continued, "that some ideas that you have about yourself are *active – dominant –* now. And these ideas are about how you or aspects of yourself have judged yourself, based on experiences in the past. If you have been unfairly accused, know that there is an aspect of yourself that is feeling guilty and judging itself. Therefore, you would have mirrors reflecting it back to you, as it happened just now with Lily. Similarly, if you have been unwelcomed, hated or have had a grudge held against you, know that an aspect of yourself is feeling unloved."

Hai San frowned down at the floor. *Is that what it is? Could Sifu be right?* He thought about his neighbour's dogs barking ceaselessly at him just now as if he were a person worthy of their contempt.

He raised his head and asked solemnly, "Sifu, if an aspect is dominant in our Personal Universe, would animals be able to detect?"

Sifu Wang threw back his head and laughed. "Got barked at by dogs, did you?"

Hai San was startled. *How could Sifu have known?*

Sifu Wang nodded sagely in understanding. "Yes, animals, especially dogs, are very sensitive. They are good mirrors for humans."

Sifu finished his drink and stood up. "Hai San, could you just walk around a bit to clear off your agitation while I make a phone call?" Sifu Wang winked at him and walked out of the room.

Hai San flushed and got up and walked around, trying to ground himself. Left foot forward, right foot forward, left foot forward, right foot forward, left foot …*Oh God, what an embarrassment! Even Sifu knows he is unhappy from his earlier skirmish with his granddaughter and Sifu's pronouncement on the aspects. It was good of Sifu to give him time to clear his agitation.*

He walked to the window and gazed out at the mango tree where he had parked his bicycle. There was a bit of breeze and he could hear the rustling of the leaves. *It's a beautiful day,* he thought. *Why am I such a grouch? Just because of two black dogs, one little girl and what Sifu said? Oh, forgive, forgive,* he can imagine Sifu saying it.

He turned from the window and walked back to his seat. He placed his two elbows on the table and cupped his chin with both palms. *Is it true that I judge myself?* He stared glumly into space. *Do I have an aspect that is feeling guilty? What is an aspect, really?* he murmured the last question aloud.

"An aspect is a Part of You," Sifu Wang replied as he walked into the room, startling Hai San, "It is a Part of You that has an issue that is unresolved. It sits within your Personal Universe with its unresolved issue seeking resolution or appeasement. As long as it remains with the unresolved issue, the Law of Mirrors will attract events or experiences of similar kind to come to you."

Hai San was perplexed. "How – how does it do that, Sifu?"

Sifu Wang sat opposite him and smiled. "Ok, let's say you had done certain things in the past where you had judged or concluded that you are 'Bad' or 'Unworthy'. Ok?"

Hai San nodded.

"So," Sifu Wang continued. "This part of yourself with its judgement of itself as 'Bad' or 'Unworthy' would have been 'frozen in time' within your Personal Universe. This 'freezing in time' is similar to saving something in a computer. Except in this case, you saved it within your Personal Universe. Now, since it is in you, you carry this Baggage around wherever you go. The Law of Mirrors will then attract similar experiences to you, where people treat you as 'Bad' or 'Unworthy' because the 'Small You' inside you believe it to be so. Do you now understand about Aspects?" Sifu Wang asked.

"Yes, Sifu." Hai San replied. "But, Sifu, if our Aspects are with us and they are such a *liability to us*, how do we get rid of them?"

"Ho, ho, ho, Hai San, you cannot really get rid of your Aspects like they are rubbish." Sifu Wang chuckled. "You see, even if your Aspects are the shadow part of you, they shouldn't be regarded a liability. They are the *hurting* and *wounded* parts of you that broke away from the core of you. They're the parts that think that they have done wrong and they're wanting to come back, to be accepted by you but they don't know *how*. They are a part of you still. So, you have to integrate them back into the Core of You. How you integrate is by breathing them in and by providing a Safe Space. Breathing enables the smooth integration. As they integrate, they release the sob stories and the erroneous conclusion and perception of who they are. In this way, your Personal Universe becomes clean and you are free of one less *baggage*."

"Oh, Sifu, can just mere breathing resolve our aspects?" Hai San asked.

Sifu Wang smiled and shook his head. "Breathing alone can't do that. You need to additionally provide *a Safe Loving Space* for your aspects to come back to. In fact, these two, Breathing and a Safe Loving Space, are important keys to achieving whatever you want."

Hai San gulped. *Breathing and A Safe Loving Space are the Secrets? And he is doing Breathing Exercises now? ....Yippee!*

TWENTY

THE STUDENT RELEASED HIS DEFENCES AROUND HIS STORIES

"Alright, Young Man, enough about Aspects and Mirrors for now. Let's get going on your experiences with the breathing exercises."

Hai San froze. His most dreaded topic had arrived. Humiliation twisted in his gut. *How was he ever going to hold up his head if he had to reveal his Big, Ugly Past to Sifu?* He inwardly cringed at the thought. He took a few deep breaths and wrung his hands nervously. He looked at Sifu with a soulful look. Sweat began pouring from his temples. His jaws tightened up. And he could hear his heart pounding in his chest.

"Well? How did your breathing exercises go?" Sifu Wang prompted.

Hai San took a few deep breaths and sighed.

Sifu Wang raised his eyebrows. "That difficult, mm?"

"Sifu, I don't know how to say it." Hai San felt stupid.

"Just start at the beginning." Sifu Wang smiled encouragingly.

"Well, mm..mmm," Hai San cleared his throat. "it's – it's like this. On the first day, I – I –" Hai San quickly took out his journal and buried his head in it.

"Nothing happened on the first day," he mumbled into the journal. "I did the breathing and felt a lot of pain. It was a kind of angry energy."

"Hmm, how did you know it was angry energy, Hai San?"

Hai San looked up from the journal. "It was intense, Sifu. It shook my pre-molar and seared my gums. I felt it circulating in my body like it was very heavy and laden."

"Interesting. Go on." Sifu Wang encouraged.

"Then, at night, I had an experience. I heard my own voice vibrating from within me, telling me to let go of my old energy." Hai San paused and peered up at Sifu Wang from his journal.

"Excellent. Go on," Sifu Wang smiled in encouragement.

"On the second day, I heard a – a voice within me saying, *'Grandpa, I've done wrong,'* But – but – it was not my own voice, Sifu."

"Oh? Whose voice did you hear, Hai San?"

"Doraemon's."

Sifu Wang chuckled and leaned back against the cushions. "Well, well. Go on."

Hai San's face went red. "After – after that, I saw a young man creeping on a rooftop. I – think I was that young man, Sifu."

Sifu Wang nodded. "Go on."

"It was dark and it seemed like there was a flood. I was trying to escape the rising waters. Then I heard moans coming from the house below me. I parted the roof tiles and saw a pregnant woman in the midst of labour. I – I – ran away. I ran away, Sifu!" Hai San broke down and covered his face with his palms.

"Calm down, Hai San. It was just a drama you had chosen to experience. That's all."

"You don't understand, Sifu. She needed help. And I just ran away. I was selfish and irresponsible."

"Hai San, don't berate yourself for whatever you think you should have done. There's a bigger picture in this than you know. Try not to be judgmental on yourself, ok?"

Hai San hastily brushed his hands over his eyes and nodded.

Sifu Wang poured more juice onto the glasses and pushed Hai San's towards him. Hai San took it immediately and gulped half of it down.

"So, what happened on the third day?"

"On the third day, I had visions of myself as a young man with a wife and child I – I – didn't love. I abandoned them to seek my fortune elsewhere. But, I died – I died – in a horrifying landslide without achieving my dreams." Hai San's voice broke as he recalled the accident that led to his death in a previous life. He took a deep breath. And another. And another. He glanced at Sifu Wang whose expression was full of understanding.

"And then?" Sifu Wang prompted.

"At night, I dreamt that my house was half buried in a landslide. I wanted to get out but I couldn't. Then, Superman appeared. But – but Superman said I was bad, irresponsible, that I wasn't worthy of rescue…" Hai San's voice tailed off in shame.

"Don't worry about it. You must love the movies, *Doraemon* and *Superman* very much to let them get into you so deeply."

"Well, I watched the movies before I did the breathing exercise, Sifu."

"I see. That accounts for their special appearance in your personal drama." Sifu Wang said with some amusement. "You know, Hai San, we all have a little Self inside of us that is very creative," Sifu Wang clarified. "This cute little Self or what psychologists call the *Inner Child* will take on any attributes that your human self is involved in and create stories out of its perception of your experiences. Because it readily absorbs what the world is about, it takes on the attributes of the world. Can you imagine, Hai San, what this means?"

Hai San shook his head.

"It means we are easily programmed, Hai San. And as easily as we are programmed, so too can each programme be overridden. They just piled up one on top of the other. Sometimes, they get mixed up like the Short Messaging Service in the handphones. So, within us is a hotchpotch of ideals, beliefs, opinions, judgments, perceptions and formulas that are as different from each other as Night and Day. Imagine, Hai San, holding such a variety of programming within us." Sifu Wang's eyes twinkled merrily.

"Over a series of many, many lifetimes, we would have developed and internalized many, many different cultures, rules and belief systems within us. If we had been a Red Indian before, we would have Red Indian rules within us. If we had been a Communist before, we would have Communist rules within us. If we had been following Hitler before, we would have Nazi rules within us. If we had been with Jesus before, we would have loving concepts within us. So, in all these, which is right and which is wrong?"

Hai San's eyes widened and he slowly shook his head.

"Exactly. There is no right or wrong, Hai San. Everything we hold within us, is just creative experience."

'Yes, Sifu."

"Good. So – let's get back to your experiences again. What happened on the fourth day?"

Hai San closed his eyes and took a few deep breaths. "On the fourth day, "he recounted slowly, his voice trembled perceptibly, "I saw visions of myself as a eunuch serving at the Chinese Imperial Palace. I was devoted to the Empress. I saw visions of court intrigues. And I burnt down the palace of one of the concubines. There was much screaming and fear." Hai San broke down and cried. "It was a most horrible and disturbing experience. I don't think I wanted to do it. But I was under instructions!"

Sifu Wang patted the young man's shoulders. "It's alright. Breathe easy. Breathe easy. Release and forgive yourself. Tell your aspect *"I AM SORRY. PLEASE FORGIVE ME. I'M SORRY THAT YOU HAVE TO UNDERGO SUCH AN EXPERIENCE. IT'S ALRIGHT. I LOVE YOU. I REALLY LOVE YOU. AND I FORGIVE YOU. ALL IS WELL.* Take a few minutes to do grounding."

Hai San took a few more deep breaths and got up to walk around the room. After a few rounds of walking and deep breathing, he took his seat again.

"Are you alright now?" Sifu Wang asked.

"Yes." He managed a smile.

"Good. Remember that all these are dramas that you chose to experience. They are neither right nor wrong. Whenever you feel bad, down and depressed, you need to practise forgiveness of your selves. To forgive is to release the judgement of apportioning blame and holding the Self responsible for a certain action. We can't ever do any wrong in God's eyes. Do you understand?

"Why not, Sifu?"

"Doing wrong is a human concept. In God's eye, we are his angels. We can't ever do wrong. Our purpose in life is to experience Self. That's all."

Hai San scratched his head in bewilderment. *He has never been wrong or guilty of anything?*

Sifu Wang smiled at his bewilderment. "Take a few deep breaths, Hai San," he instructed.

Hai San did as instructed.

"Now, make yourself comfortable. The idea of forgiveness is best explained from the parable of the Prodigal Son," Sifu Wang clarified.

"The Prodigal Son? Is that a story, Sifu?" Hai San asked.

"Yes, it's a story told by Jesus and it explains the real meaning of forgiveness. Now, I'm not telling you this to make you into a Christian but to show you what it means to forgive. Ok?"

"Ok, Sifu," Hai San answered readily, eager to hear the story.

Sifu Wang smiled. "Well, the story of the Prodigal Son tells us of a Father who had two sons. When they were old enough, he gave them each a part of his wealth and told them to use it as they deem fit. One son left the home and made his way into the world, spending his inheritance as he liked, enjoying life with wine, women and song and before long, all his money had been spent. The other one remained with the father and did his so-called duty by being obedient and never spending unless it was absolutely necessary. So when the son who had left home found that all his money had been used up, he returned home, hoping to seek refuge with his father. He was welcomed back heartily by the father and feted like a long lost son. The other son, having remained obedient and dutiful, was not happy that such a wastrel brother was welcomed back as if he had not done any wrong. He went to the father to complain but instead, the father taught him the meaning of forgiveness, that every child to him is an angel and by that very fact, can never do any wrong." Sifu Wang explained.

"So, what is the moral of the story, Sifu?" Hai San frowned in confusion.

"The moral of the story is that God wishes us to be like him, to treat every person with forgiveness, meaning that we should view every person we meet as if he is an angel, just like us, and therefore can do no wrong. Thus, forgiveness is not that we release a person from responsibility or blame but that we view him as an angel and therefore, he is not blame-able in the first place. Do you understand?"

"Yes, I think so. But how do we forgive ourselves, Sifu?" Hai San asked.

"Well, you bring yourselves, the selves that you see from your previous lives into your mind's eye and tell them this, '*You are an angel. I know you could do no wrong. And you haven't.*' Can you do that, Hai San?"

"Oh, yes, Sifu. That's easy enough," Hai San replied.

"Good," Sifu Wang said approvingly. "So, what happened on the fifth day?"

"Well, on the fifth day, I saw visions of myself as a Red Indian Chief leading my warriors across some rugged countryside to reach our camp. It appeared that we were too late. The next vision I saw was the remains of a devastated camp. Everybody was dead, including my wives and kids. I was – inconsolable," Hai San finished off in a flat tone.

"And you have also been guilty ever since," Sifu Wang concluded.

"Yes," Hai San whispered, his throat tightening up.

"Forget it, Hai San. We didn't come into this world to fix it. We came to experience, to give ourselves *creative flow* and – *creative expression*. Do you understand?"

"Yes, Sifu."

"Good. Don't be too tied up with all your stories and judgments of right and wrong," Sifu Wang advised. "Those dramas are just parts that you chose to play to understand yourself better. You need to do your forgiveness exercise regularly, Young Man."

"Alright, Sifu," Hai San replied.

"What happened on the sixth day?" Sifu Wang asked.

"On the sixth day, I saw myself as a crazy dominican nun. I – I think I enrolled at the convent after a failed love affair. I behaved like the whole world was my enemy. I talked and laughed to myself and frightened other nuns with my weird habits. Even visiting priests and benefactors were not spared." Hai San wrung his hands in agitation.

"Hmm, what happened to you afterwards? Was there any conclusion?" Sifu Wang asked.

Hai San looked down glumly and sniffed.

"It's ok," Sifu Wang consoled. "You just need to release yourself from all the unhappy feelings you have accumulated within you. Therefore, you must continually practise forgiveness and letting go."

"They imprisoned me in a cell for months, Sifu. The vision was one of darkness, continual darkness. I probably died there," Hai San revealed.

"It's ok. It's over, Hai San. It was an unhappy experience. But it's over. You have to let it go." Sifu Wang placed a comforting hand on Hai San's shoulders.

Hai San took a few deep breaths and managed a smile.

"I'm done with it, Sifu."

"Good, good. So, what happened on the seventh day, Young Man?"

"On the seventh day, I saw myself as a lady, a French lady, I think, in what looked like nineteenth century England. Outwardly, I was a beautiful upper class lady, on a tour of England but in reality I was a spy. I lured men to reveal their political secrets in a most shameful way. In the end, I was shot dead by a man I had betrayed."

"And the eightth day?"

"I was a stupid and corrupt ruler in some place that feels like Africa. I misused the funds of my kingdom to support my wives. I had hundreds of wives, you see, and they were always demanding for money, gifts...I had visions of invasion by white man and being killed." Hai San said.

"Interesting," Sifu Wang said smilingly. "Go on."

Hai San looked down into his journal. He remained silent for a while. Then he looked up at Sifu and asked, "Sifu, can I skip to tell you about the tenth day?"

Sifu Wang raised an eyebrow. "Skip? Why, what's so *different* about the ninth day?"

"Er, on the ninth day, I – I was a – a – " Hai San's face turned red. He buried his face into his journal. He had never been so ashamed.

Sifu Wang looked at him curiously and with dawning realisation, chuckled. "Go on," he prompted.

"I – I – was a – a –" Hai San just could not get the words out.

"A – cabaret dancer, B- prostitute, C – courtesan, D – concubine?" Sifu Wang supplied the options. "Which is it?'

Hai San nearly jumped. He looked at Sifu Wang with surprise. *How did Sifu know?*

Sifu Wang grinned. "Hai San, we've all been on our rounds. Almost every role that the world has to offer, we've been in it. It's our Creative Self again. We crave experiences, you see. And we wanted to know what it's like to be born in a certain situation, in a certain family and to take on certain roles and experiences. Believe me, this is *nothing new*."

"You mean, Sifu, that you were also a...a professional entertainer before?" Hai San asked incredulously.

Sifu Wang laughed heartily. "I was once the favourite courtesan of a king in Ancient Egypt. The scene I remember was something that could have been carved out of the Arabian Nights. I was not only beautiful but intelligent as well. I could recite poetry, sing, dance and keep the king entertained in all manner of things for weeks and months on end. But, in the end, because of what I was and what I could do, I was poisoned to death."

"Oh! Oh, how sad, Sifu!" Hai San's face nearly crumbled at the thought of such a dreadful end.

"Not at all. If I hadn't been poisoned, the king would have lost his kingdom. He had become weak because of his infatuation with me. That would have been disastrous for his people."

"So, who poisoned you, Sifu?"

"Why, the Queen and his Minister collaborated to finish me off," Sifu Wang said cheerfully.

"Oh. I still think it's sad."

Sifu Wang ruffled Hai San's hair. "You are sentimental, Young Man. So what were you before?"

Hai San gave a sheepish grin. "I was a *B*, Sifu."

Sifu Wang laughed out heartily. Things were looking not so bad on him after all.

"So, let's get on with your experiences."

"Ok." Hai San said with great relief. He looked into his journal and recounted, "Well, on the tenth day, I saw myself as a scientist doing some experiments in an underground laboratory. I was obsessive about my work. I had visions of arguments. Lots of them – with what looks like government people and fellow scientists. The next vision I had were two cities being bombed and destroyed. I felt darkness entering my life. I was never the same after that."

"Hmm, any more?"

"No, that's all, Sifu."

"Great. Well done, Hai San. Now, tell me, what have you learnt from all these visions and dreams?

Hai San thought for a while before answering. "Sifu, I was many different personalities with different life paths."

"Excellent observation! We all don different costumes, play different roles, live in different environments and undergo different challenges in the course of our incarnations. So, in one lifetime, we may be a Caucasian, in another a Negro, a Malay, a Chinese, an Indian. You name it, we have been in many ethnic groups and in many different places in different lifetimes. What we call 'birth' is in reality a beginning of an earth drama and 'death' is the end of it. Our consciousness, our spirit, our I AM, lives on and never dies. We are eternal. We are all Angels."

"So, what is the purpose of all these incarnations, Sifu?"

"To understand ourselves better, Hai San, and to unlock a critical situation that was created hundreds of millions of years ago."

"Oh, what is that, Sifu?" Hai San was curious.

"Well," Sifu Wang looked at his student with amusement. "We are all Consciousness working with Energy, Hai San. And Consciousness is Creative. At one point before Earth began, something happened in the Multi-verses that got it stuck, you see. Exactly how, I'm not too sure. I guess a great amount of Fear and Manipulation of Consciousness was involved that created this event. So, to release this stuck energy, it was decided by the Councils in Heaven to create a small experimental realm of limitation and to call for volunteers, the Children of God, to play in this experimental playground to understand how to work with energy and resolve the situation that got stuck. That's how Earth came to be created and how we are here again and again to solve the great mystery."

"So, that's why we play in different dramas, to understand what we can do?"

"Yes. And we voluntarily forgot our true divine heritage so that we could move one hundred per cent into the roles that we play."

"So, what do I do now, Sifu? How shall I continue with my life?" Hai San asked anxiously.

"The training of the Secrets is meant to awaken the Divinity inside of you, Hai San. Once the Divine in You is awakened, you will have all the resources of the universe supporting you. You will know that you are a very powerful person, different from others. No longer will you feel like an ordinary person nor act like one. You would be able to command and make things happen effortlessly." Sifu Wang explained.

"How will I be different, Sifu? Will I become abnormal?" Hai San asked worriedly.

Sifu Wang threw back his head and laughed.

"Am I abnormal, Hai San?" Sifu Wang asked, with laughter lingering in his eyes.

"No, Sifu," Hai San grinned. "But what about my family, friends, sports activities and other interests? Will I continue to have them?"

"*If* you choose to. You can continue having any or all of those things. What I mean is that you will view events and experiences from a totally different perspective of SELF. You will discover the magnificence of Who and What you are and What you can do. In the discovery, you will become a Leader among Men and a Grand Example for Others to follow. Other people may moan and grumble about their lives, issues and experiences. They may speculate, blame and gossip about things and people. But you will not. You will not be involved in any of these dramas anymore. Instead, you will take Total Responsibility for Self. Because you are a Master, a Sovereign of your own Universe, you know all you need is to take charge and command and things will just happen for you, like this." Sifu Wang snapped his fingers.

"Wow – I will be a Super Being?" Hai San's eyes gleamed in anticipation.

"Yes, Hai San. You will be a Super Being." Sifu Wang confirmed.

TWENTY-ONE

THE STUDENT LEARNT THE IMPORTANCE OF CREATING A SAFE HAVEN

'You will view events and experiences from a totally different perspective of SELF. You will discover the magnificence of Who and What you are and What you can do. In the discovery, you will become a Grand Example for Others to follow.'

Hai San smiled to himself as he recalled Sifu's words. Oh how grand life would be then. He couldn't wait for his Mastery. If he had a choice, he wanted all the Magnificence NOW. But Sifu had said many a time, "Be patient, Hai San. Whatever you want to achieve cannot be done overnight."

A heavy hand descended upon Hai San's shoulders. Hai San jumped and swerved round.

"Ken Chye!" he exclaimed in surprise. But whatever he wanted to say got stuck in his throat. Surprise erupted into shock. His usually debonair 'smart Alec' friend now not only looked pale and wan, but thoroughly dishevelled as well, as if a major tragedy had befallen him the night before.

"Ken Chye," Hai San repeated, concern colouring his voice. "What's wrong? You – don't look – well."

"There's no need to be *that* polite." His friend glared at him. "I feel and look terrible, I know," he added with a grimace.

Hai San raised his brows. "Yeah, Friend – you need – er – valet service." He suddenly chuckled, overcome by his own amusement.

Ken Chye glared at him again before looking around and moving away out of the hearing of other students. Hai San followed him.

They stopped under an angsana tree, facing the football field. "It's my Mum." Ken Chye said gruffly after a while, swallowing the lump in his throat. He stood, uncertainly, his eyes dazed. "I – I'm worried about her."

"Oh?" Hai San was puzzled. The last time he had seen Ken Chye's mother, she had looked happy and recovered.

"You remember her appointment with Sifu Wang, don't you?" his friend asked.

"Yes, but I thought she's already ok. She looked fine to me." Hai San frowned as he tried to recall a bit further of his encounter with Madam Tang.

"Yeah – well – she was ok – "Ken Chye admittedly slowly, "before the appointment."

"You mean she is not ok *now*?" Hai San prompted.

"Yes – what I mean is – she is behaving out of sorts now. I don't know what was said at the appointment, Hai San. All I know is that she is not herself." Ken Chye revealed, blinking his eyes rapidly and fighting back tears.

Hai San patted his friend's shoulders consolingly. "Tell me what happened," he urged quietly.

Ken Chye sighed. He had run through the sequence of events in his mind far too many times. What was one more if Hai San could help unravel the mystery? "She went out for breakfast with Sifu on Saturday," he recounted. "When she came back, she shut herself in her room for hours. When she came out, her eyes were all red and puffy. I know she had been crying. Now a few days have passed and she is barely talking. I hope it's not any bad news from Sifu." Ken Chye looked ahead bleakly.

"Regarding her illness, you mean?" Hai San asked, risking a look at his friend.

Ken Chye nodded. He kicked at a stone which went flying into a nearby drain. Both boys were silent for a while, trying to grapple with the ramifications if Madam Tang's illness were to deteriorate into the dreaded disease once again. Unwelcome as it was, it could be a likely event.

"I'm so afraid, Hai San," Ken Chye admitted in a low voice.

"Nothing will happen to her, Ken Chye," Hai San assured his friend kindly.

"I have never been more scared in my life," his friend continued as if he hadn't spoken. "I don't know what I'll do if – if something happens to my Mum," Ken Chye's voice broke. He plopped down onto a nearby bench and cradled his head in his hands.

"Come on, nothing will happen to her." Hai San sat down beside his friend. "Look, how about I discuss this with Sifu? I'm sure Sifu will be able to advise us."

Ken Chye lifted his head and stared at his friend curiously. "Isn't there such a thing as patient's confidentiality?"

"Sure. But your Mum's case is different. We're all involved right at the very beginning, weren't we? It's not as if we were kept unaware all along. Besides," Hai San continued confidently, "I'm a Trainee with Sifu. I need to know in order to learn how to handle a situation such as this, in the future."

Ken Chye took a deep audible breath and smiled slowly, his eyes brightening up. "If you're sure it's ok, Hai San. Thanks – thanks a lot. I feel so much better already."

"Hei, what are friends for?" Hai San grinned, giving his friend a reassuring squeeze and then a punch on the shoulder.

• • •

The ceiling fan made swishing sounds as the blades rotated. The day had been warm when they started the lesson. The air conditioner had broken down and Sifu Wang had jokingly said that it was a result of all the energy expansion and release done by Hai San, It was a good thing that the fan was still functional. Now Sifu Wang was talking about the significance of breathing again. Hai San contemplated about how he was going to ask Sifu about Madam Tang. He now realized that it was not as easy as he had assured his friend it would be. On hindsight, Ken Chye could be right. A patient's confidentiality was something that needed to be kept and which he had never seriously thought about.

"We're finished for the day, Hai San," Sifu's voice seemed to snap him back to attention.

"Huh? Sorry, Sifu." Hai San looked embarrassed. "I'm sorry I wasn't paying attention."

"Hmm. A lot seemed to occupy your mind, Hai San. Anything I could help you with?" Sifu Wang smiled questioningly at his student. He was anything but displeased.

"Er…yes, Sifu…" Hai San replied haltingly. He was unsure as to how he could bring up the subject matter of Madam Tang without appearing a busybody.

"Yes?" Sifu prompted, smilingly.

"It's Ken Chye, Sifu. He – he's worried about his mother," Hai San revealed.

"Ah – I see." Sifu Wang nodded sagely. "Why is your friend worried about his mother?"

"He says his mother doesn't appear to be – er – happy. She is not talking to him like usual and he – he's afraid that – you may have given her bad news about her illness." There, it was all out and Hai San felt greatly relieved. He darted a look at his teacher.

Sifu just smiled. *What does that mean?*

"Er – Sifu, what do I tell Ken Chye?" Hai San probed.

Sifu stroked his chin while he considered the issue. Then he said, "Hai San, there are some things you need to know about your *heritage* if you are to be a healing facilitator in future."

Hai San's eyes rounded while he waited for his teacher to continue.

"You have gone through a series of breathing exercises, haven't you?" Sifu Wang asked him.

"Yes, Sifu," Hai San replied.

"And you have seen the many different personalities of Your Self, haven't you?"

"Yes, Sifu."

"Good. Do you know where these parts of Your Self reside?"

Hai San frowned. They were talking about Madam Tang and what he should tell Ken Chye. *Why was Sifu asking him about his breathing exercises?*

He took a deep breath and answered, "Within us. I mean, in our Personal Universe, Sifu"

"Excellent! You've understood your lesson well." Sifu Wang nodded approvingly. "We carry them in our Personal Universe. They are our Unfinished and Unresolved Business, Hai San. They are the Parts of Us that have unhappy or unsatisfactory experiences and are unfulfilled. We carry them with us, life after life because they are our Creation in Illusion. When conditions are conducive, these parts of us come forward and compel us to confront them. So – how is this related to Madam Tang, you may ask?" Sifu asked smilingly.

Hai San jerked in surprise. *Had Sifu read his thoughts?*

"What Madam Tang experienced as cancer," Sifu Wang continued, "was nothing more than the result of physical blockage caused by the parts of Herself that have unresolved issues and are actively seeking resolution. What I merely did was to disperse this physical blockage. When the blockage disappeared, the cancer also disappeared. But that was only a temporary measure, Hai San. To permanently heal, each person must personally be responsible for integrating the Separated Parts of Himself back into Wholeness. So, what is within Madam Tang, she personally must resolve and re-integrate into her Self. I can't do that for her," Sifu Wang said.

"But, can you teach her, Sifu?" Hai San appealed.

"Sure, Hai San. But, unfortunately," Sifu Wang continued regretfully, shaking his head, "like most people, she prefers a quick fix. She thinks it's a matter of getting rid of the symptoms. And that she can relegate the healing to another person."

"Sifu, you said the blockage has disappeared. Isn't that good enough?" Hai San asked earnestly.

"No, it's never enough, Hai San. Don't you know that cancer will recur time and time again?"

"Yes, I've heard about that. Why is that, Sifu?"

"Unfinished business, Hai San. When we disperse a blockage, the stuck energy causing the blockage temporarily moves away. But it's still within the Personal Universe, you see. As long as it is not resolved, it will come back again seeking resolution. If not in this life, then in the next life or the life after next."

"Why, Sifu? Why does that happen?"

"The created belongs to the Creator. So they will always come back to the Creator seeking resolution and unity."

"Oh." Hai San frowned and scratched his head. *Sifu's explanation is too abstract.*

Sifu Wang smiled at his expression.

"We are Creators, Hai San. Every experience that we have is experienced by an aspect of our self. Each aspect has its own Story to tell. Some have angry stories while others have fear, unhappiness, regrets, guilt, dissatisfaction, you name it…" Sifu Wang explained.

"Each Aspect longs to come back to the fold, to be united with the Self. But it can't do that unless it feels safe, loved and cared for. So the Self needs to provide a Save Haven for the aspects to come back.

"So how do we provide a Safe Haven, Sifu?"

"We can only provide a safe haven, Hai San, if we let go of all our criticisms, our scolding, our judgements and perceptions of right and wrong. The feeling that we should have is : It doesn't matter. It is alright. I love you all the same. With that feeling, we *breathe,* Hai San, and *feel compassion* for our Aspects. We may feel their pain and their anguish and all we need do is to be with IT and have Total Allowance and Acceptance for IT."

"But how? If we breathe and feel, won't we be affected by the old stories and the anger, the guilt, the sadness and so on?"

Sifu Wang chuckled. His student seemed to have a good grasp of the subject. "We will feel the pain and the anguish of our Aspects but we are GODS, right?"

Hai San nodded.

"When we own up to our Divinity, acting like the God that we are, without judgement and having Compassion and Unconditional Love for our puny human self and aspects, everything we say and do has Magic," Sifu Wang declared.

Hai San's eyes widened in surprise. He felt his heart skip a beat.

"When the God that we are is Present, something Extraordinary will be bound to happen. Our Aspects will begin integrating with Us, one by one," Sifu Wang continued.

"Oh, Sifu, it seems so easy. But does it really work? And *how*?" Hai San asked his teacher avidly.

Sifu Wang's eyes gleamed. "Hai San, when we do our breathing and are totally relaxed, providing a safe haven for our aspects, the minute the aspects integrate with us, we will know. It's like a bubble bursting, a release and a feeling of ecstasy. Why don't you just do it, Hai San? Then you tell me if it works. Magic is – Magic. There's nothing to explain. It needs to be experienced."

"Alright!" Hai San exclaimed and clasped his hands together excitedly. "I'm going to do it, Sifu!"

"Good!" Sifu Wang nodded with approval. "But, don't forget about our dear friend."

Hai San scratched his head. "Who?"

"Who else?" Sifu Wang asked quizzically.

"Oh – oh – Madam Tang?"

"Naturally. Get her son to be involved as well. I'm sure you young men can help to convince her of the importance of self-healing. It doesn't make sense to carry a big baggage of *yesterdays* around, right?"

"Right!" Hai San smiled widely. He was beginning to get excited.

• • •

TWENTY-TWO

THE STUDENT PLAYED THE TEACHER

Hai San drew his bicycle outside the gate of Ken Chye's house and rang his bicycle bell. Then, he waited for his friend to appear. A few seconds later, his friend came hurrying from the direction of the back door.

"Hei, Ken Chye! Still not ready yet?"

"Shshhh!" Ken Chye tried to silence his friend.

Hai San wordlessly gestured *'what's the big deal?'*.

"My mum's inside," his friend whispered. "I'll see you at Mamak Stall in, say, another ten minutes, ok?"

"K!" Hai San said cheerfully, steering his bicycle away in the direction of Mamak Stall.

Ten minutes later, Hai San gaped in horrified silence as he watched his friend gobbled up the food like a man who had been starved for days.

Ken Chye lifted up his head and spied his friend watching him. "Haven't seen me eating before?" he rasped out.

"Sorry," Hai San chuckled. "It fascinates me, that's all. You eat like – er – you haven't eaten for days."

"I haven't," Ken Chye admitted, after swallowing a mouthful of the delicious noodles.

"What – your Mum took leave from the kitchen?" Hai San jested.

Ken Chye shook his head. "Naw, her food was just awful. I ate a bare minimum everyday and threw away the rest."

"But your Mum is a great cook, Ken Chye!" Hai San was shocked. He just could not believe what his friend was saying.

"Yeah, don't I know it! But what she's been dishing out these days are not worth eating," Ken Chye said with a shrug and continued gobbling up the remaining noodles on his plate.

"How can you say that of your own Mother?" Hai San shook his head in disgust.

"Friend, have you ever eaten food that tastes flat? Soup without salt or seasoning? Or chicken that is partially cooked?" Ken Chye asked grittily, his eyes getting redder by the minute.

"Oh, no. Is this what is happening?" Hai San's eyes widened.

"Yes." Ken Chye sniffed. "I'm losing her everyday, Hai San. She – she –" Ken Chye's voice broke and he lifted up his arm to wipe his eyes against his sleeve.

"Oh, Ken Chye, I'm sure everything will work out soon." Hai San reached out to comfort his friend.

Ken Chye hunched his shoulders and frowned miserably into the distance, oblivious to the activities of the hawker stall. Hai San felt terrible for his friend. Madam Tang was a woman in her early 40s, quite pretty in appearance and still very much in her prime if she makes an effort. How sad it must be to be so resistant to changes, to accept nobody's ideas except her own and then having had to face her challenges all alone, with nobody to confide in and share her troubles. And Ken Chye was at a loss as to how to handle the situation with his mother.

After what seemed like a long silence, Hai San said quietly, "I spoke to Sifu yesterday."

His friend lifted up his head with a gleam in his eyes and asked, "What did he say?"

"Sifu said we can help."

"We? As in *You* and *I*?" Ken Chye queried.

"Yes, Sifu said to also get you involved."

"He said that? But how?" Ken Chye was puzzled.

"It's quite an explanation. Are you sure you're up to it?"

"I'm all ears, Friend." Excitement crept into his voice. He levered himself upright, leaned back and said with typical Ken Chye arrogance, "Don't keep me waiting."

Hai San laughed. Now his friend sounded like he was back to normal. Shucks, he hated all kinds of upsets and the last few days of seeing his friend's strange and unhappy mood was enough to send cold shivers down his spine.

"Sifu explained that we all carry unresolved Parts of Ourselves within us. These parts of Ourselves have their Stories rooted in sadness, fear, anger or unfulfilment," Hai San said, looking at his friend to see whether he was following.

"Go on," Ken Chye indicated.

"At certain times in our life, when the conditions are activated, these Parts of Us will confront us, seeking resolution. If we don't do anything about them, they will eventually create a blockage in our body and cause Dis-ease."

"So, let me get it right – what you are saying is that when my Mum had cancer, she was confronted with a Part of Herself that was unhappy, angry or unfulfilled and seeking Resolution?"

"Yes, exactly!"

"But she doesn't have cancer now. So where did that Part go to, hmm?""

"It moves around but is still within her Personal Universe, Ken Chye."

"Her what???"

"Personal Universe. Our personal universe is our own private world seen and experienced from our own perspective, Ken Chye. It contains everything that we are, our perceptions, ideas, beliefs and understanding of issues, people and situations and our relationship and connections with the rest of the world," Hai San explained. "When a Part of Our Self is angry, sad or unfulfilled and remained unresolved, It cannot remain in that condition forever. Even as It floats around in our Personal Universe, there will come a time when It must come back to us seeking Resolution. As It does, It sits within us causing a blockage. Cancer is the physical result when that Part of Us desperately seeks resolution and we are not allowing it the resolution it seeks. The energy of the Unresolved Self becomes aggressive in its intent."

"I see. So what is your advice, Doctor?" Ken Chye asked.

"Don't you believe me?" Hai San stared into his friend's eyes. "Or Sifu?"

"Sure, I believe you. But what's the Solution, Doctor?"

"Do lots of Breathing."

"Hah!" Ken Chye got up abruptly from his seat, paused, then snatched up his tea which had grown cold and drained it in a long gulp.

"I've got to go," he flung the words at his friend.

"There's something more, of course. But, friend, you won't get it from me in this mood. If you love your Mum, you jolly well sit down again and listen," Hai San said dryly, leaning back and spearing his eyes at Ken Chye.

"Huh?" Ken Chye was nonplussed. Hai San had never spoken to him in that manner before. He dropped back onto his seat.

Hai San allowed himself a little grin. It takes psychology to manage his friend.

"Sifu will teach, of course. But your Mum needs to be convinced."

"What do you mean?"

"Sifu says your Mum is not open to the idea of self-healing. She doesn't believe much in Breathing as a healing technique. But I have personally experienced relief from blockages caused by my many, many aspects of myself and I vouch for it. Breathing works! You can feel bliss when you breathe sufficiently. Breathing clears the clutter. And it clears the pain, the anger and the fear in our body. It straightens out not just the knots in our body but also in our life. Above all, it manifests whatever we desire in our life," Hai San pointed out to his friend.

Ken Chye gaped at Hai San with amazement. How profound Hai San sounded. *How did he know these things? What had his friend been doing while he, Ken Chye, moved around daily in blissful ignorance?*

"Well, well," Ken Chye mocked. "For a moment I thought you had transformed into Sifu,".

Hai San shook his head and chuckled. "So, do you think you can convince your Mum to go for self-healing, Ken Chye?"

Ken Chye shook his head slowly. He knew his own Mother. If there is a prize for stubbornness, his Mum will win it, hands down. *So what is this about Breathing? Why is it so important? And can it really heal?* He thought about Sifu Wang. Sifu looked young and healthy although he must be in his sixties. And he was vitally alive unlike some men his age. In fact, Sifu had the body of a man half his age and without a grey hair on his head.

There must be some truth in his healing method. But his Mum ... his Mum was another person altogether. She was not easy to convince. He stared unseeingly into the distance. What he required was *strategy*. But *what* and *how*? He pursed his lips and tapped his fingers restlessly on the makeshift table.

Hai San cocked his head at his friend. "So – got any answers yet? How do you intend to convince your Mum?"

"Let me think," Ken Chye replied. His head was feeling heavy and he felt the onset of a headache. He sat engrossed for a few minutes. Then, all of a sudden, he had a brainwave. He banged his fist on the table top so hard that a saucer jumped.

Hai San's eyes rounded. When his friend behaved in this manner, he surely had a 5 star strategy.

"I have it!" Ken Chye declared and laughed with glee.

"What? Do tell, Ken Chye!" Hai San begged. He was getting as excited as his friend.

"It's like this," Ken Chye's eyes shone with triumph. "I'll strike a deal with my Mum."

"A deal?" Hai San was suddenly doubtful.

"Yes, listen. This is what I'm going to do. I'm going to tell my Mum that if she doesn't follow Sifu's instructions to heal herself, I will have no choice but to leave school and go to work with my Uncle John to help supplement the family income. After all, if something happens to her, who is going to take care of my sister and me? In fact, I'll have to start doing it now."

"You can't do that! You have to finish school." Hai San was aghast.

"It's only a bluff, Hai San! I will need to be convincing, though. That's where you come in. I need you to back me up."

"I don't know, Ken Chye. It doesn't sound right," Hai San replied, frowning doubtfully at his friend.

"Then you tell me what sounds right," his friend demanded. "You want to wait for my Mum to die first before you would help me, right?"

"That's not true!" Hai San protested.

"So, say you'll help," Ken Chye demanded.

"Alright," Hai San conceded reluctantly. "But don't go overboard with your schemes, ok?"

"Not to worry, Friend!" Ken Chye grinned.

• • •

Hai San breathed in deeply. And breathed out deeply. For the two hundredth time or so it seemed. He had been doing the breathing exercise for two days now. And he was bored with it. *Oh why does Sifu have to give him this breathing exercise? Why? Why? Why?*

All of a sudden, he felt his heart and solar plexus opened up. And his body started to relax in a way that he had never before experienced. It was as if Something was poured from Somewhere into his entire being and the aches and pains he had had for the past two days just melted and disappeared miraculously without trace. Oh, how cool! How cool! He allowed his body to relax and absorb the Whatever that was coming in.

He continued his breathing. In . Out. In. Out. In. Out. In. Out. In. Out. In. Out. He could hardly feel his body now. So relaxed. So relaxed. Now he was One with the Universe. *Flowing with It. Flowing with It. Rhythmically.* In. Out. In. Out. In. Out. In. Out. Time no longer existed. Space no longer existed. There was only Him. Only the One. In. Out. In. Out. In. Out.

A dog barked in the distance. There was the sound of a gate closing noisily. Hai San cocked his ear for his neighbour's voice. Then he became aware of his head. His body. His toes. Just like that, he's back. He's back!

What an experience...! He must share it with Sifu.

• • •

Rrring.........Rrring....Rrring .... Rrring......Rrring........

Hai San waited at the gate for his friend to appear. When his friend showed no sign of appearing, he gave a loud whistle. A curtain moved and Madam Tang peeped out.

Hai San lifted his arm and waved. Madam Tang gave a half smile and a negative wave, indicating that Ken Chye was not at home.

Funny, where could Ken Chye be after being absent from school for two days? Hai San thought. He turned his bicycle around as if to head back home, then thought better of it and rang his bicycle bell again. "Auntie!" he shouted.

Madam Tang peeped out through the windows again. "Yes, anything, Hai San?" She shouted back.

Hai San got down from his bicycle and took out a folder from his carrier. Madam Tang came walking out reluctantly to the gate, looking pitifully wan.

"What is it, Hai San?" she asked wearily.

"School assignments, Auntie. Since Ken Chye was absent for two days, I thought I'll pass him the school assignments."

"Absent? *Absent*, you say?" Madam Tang asked with disbelief. "Ken Chye was absent from school for two days?" she repeated, her voice shrilled out to almost a hysterical level.

"Yes…" Hai San's voice tailed off when he realized that something was wrong. *Oh no, had his friend started doing his deal with his mother?* Hai San shook his head to get a grip on himself.

Madan Tang closed her eyes and placed a hand at her temple in obvious distress. She swayed for a few seconds.

Hai San reached out to steady her. "Auntie! Are you alright?"

Madam Tang shook her head silently as her eyes glazed over. She swayed again and gripped the gate to steady herself. Hai San inwardly cursed Ken Chye for putting him in this situation.

"Auntie, let me help you inside." Hai San opened the gate and gently walked Madam Tang back into her house. As soon as she was inside, she slid onto the floor and let out a low wailing sound, as if in great pain. Hai San shuddered and quickly closed the door for fear of arousing the neighbors' curiosity.

He looked at Madam Tang's curled up figure pitifully. *Oh, what should he do now? What should he do now?* he asked himself frantically. *Where are you, Ken Chye? Where are you, dammit! Don't place me in this situation!*

Madam Tang was weeping, with an arm thrown across her face. From time to time, she gave a low moan as if in pain.

Hai San hovered helplessly a few meters away. He felt positively surreal – he had never encountered such a situation before and he was at a lost as to what he should do. Finally, he took a deep breath for courage and slowly walked over, crouched down and placed a sympathetic hand on Madam Tang's shoulder.

"Auntie, it's ok. I'll go find Ken Chye. I'm sure he is somewhere around. I'll get him back," he told her assuringly.

Madam Tang looked up at him wordlessly with soulful, tearful eyes and began to weep again.

Hai San looked on in frustration. Then he quickly strode into the kitchen. Within a couple of minutes, he came back with a glass of warm honey and handed it to Madam Tang. She looked at him and the glass of honey and finally lifted her hand to take it from him. She placed the glass on the small coffee table before wiping her eyes with her T-shirt. "You – you're – a good boy, Hai San," she whispered brokenly.

"Auntie, don't worry about Ken Chye. I'm sure he has a good reason for not going to school."

"Hai San, how can I not worry?" she cried out, her voice stronger now. "School boys should go to school. That is their duty. If they're not in school, they must be out roaming the streets and getting into bad company."

"Ken Chye is not like that, Auntie. I'll help you find him. Now you please take your drink and relax. I'll get him back for you." Hai San tried his best to reassure his friend's Mother.

Madam Tang was silent for a while. She stared unseeingly into space then let out a long grateful sigh. "Thank you. Thank you, Hai San."

• • •

Hai San cycled off from Ken Chye's house as if he was hounded by a rottweiler. He headed straight for John's Spare Parts Shop at Paya Terubong.

On arrival, he quickly strode to the backyard where repairs of cars were ongoing. A few mechanics were at work, fiddling with the engines of cars while at the far end, it appears a group of three men were in discussion beside an old Mercedes Benz. Hai San approached the group quietly and one of them, Ken Chye's uncle, turned his head to look at him. He broke into a smile and lifted a hand in greeting. Hai San greeted him back in similar manner.

Where is Ken Chye? Hai San took a quick sweeping look over the garage and finally spied a pair of legs stretched out from underneath a car, clad in what looks like Ken Chye's cut off jeans. He went over and kicked hard at the shins. A loud swearing rang out from beneath the engines.

"Get out! Damn you – Ken Chye!" Hai San was angry.

A few seconds later, his friend dragged his thin body out from under the car. He palmed his injured legs and glared at Hai San. "Do you have to be so rough?"

"Don't you think you deserve it?" Hai San took a step forward and glowered at his friend.

"Ok, ok…" Ken Chye took a step backward and raised his arms in defence. "I'm sorry, ok?"

Hai San drew in a few deep breaths to calm himself. The air in and around the garage smelled of grease and fumes.

"Your Mum is distraught. I think you should go back home, Ken Chye. She was crying and wailing a full half hour just now when she realized you haven't been attending school."

Ken Chye grimaced. "You know the objective."

"But not in this way – are you mad?"

"Then what way?" What way, smart guy?" Ken Chye demanded.

Hai San took a step forward and grabbed his friend by the collar. "Next time you need to talk to your Mother, don't involve me in your scheme. I don't like to deal with a weeping woman. She Is Your Mother. You Find Your Own Solution." Then he let go of Ken Chye's collar.

Ken Chye adjusted his collar and said adamantly, "This is *the* Solution. *The Only Solution*, Friend." Then his voice broke into a sob.

Hai San's anger abated instantly. He felt like a heel for treating his friend so badly when the latter was facing the biggest emotional challenge of his life. He stepped forward to apologise. "Ken Chye, I –"

His friend looked up from wiping his eyes with his t-shirt. "I'm going home now. Will you come with me?"

Hai San cringed at the thought of a confrontation. His immediate reflex was to say *no*. Then he looked at his friend's miserable face and defeated stance. *Oh, what the hack! What is one more drama to complete the day?*

• • •

TWENTY-THREE

THE STUDENTS BEGAN CONSCIOUS BREATHING

The greatest challenge of the year was convincing Madam Tang to self-heal. After Sifu Wang's activation of her chakras, she had felt wonderfully fit and strong without any of the pain that had previously caused her to double up in agony. So why should she even consider self-healing when healing was not needed? As to the possibility of relapse, she would only cross the bridge when she came to it. For the meantime, she resolved that she would not be so easily frightened. Thus, it was with much difficulty that both boys had tried to plead with her to self-heal but to no avail. Instead, Ken Chye had got the brunt of his mother's anger for playing truant from school and Hai San had to promise Madam Tang to report on his friend if he ever repeated the offence in the future.

So both boys went back to their normal routine with heavy hearts, leaving the unsatisfactory episode behind them.

Three weeks later, Madam Tang was mopping up her kitchen floor when she felt a dull piercing sensation in her abdomen. A sliver of fear ran through her body as she immediately discarded her mop and sat on her kitchen stool, trying to grasp the ramifications of this new pain. Sifu Wang's words rang through her mind.

"The blockage in your liver may have disappeared. But their energy hasn't. Right now, my guess is they're circulating within your energy field. One day they're going to settle somewhere and cause a blockage again if you don't do anything to resolve them now."

Her whole body went cold. *Surely,…surely she was not going to have a relapse?*

She felt the panic rising within her again. *Oh, what was she going to do?* She trembled as she thought of her life, her dreams and her ambitions for her children peter away to nothing if she were afflicted with the Disease again.

So, it was a silent and sober mum that Ken Chye returned to from sports that evening. After dinner, while his younger sister was playing at her computer, Madam Tang sat down Ken Chye in the living room and asked him the ALL IMPORTANT QUESTION.

"Kenny, do you think you could ask Hai San to fix a session for me with Sifu? I'm considering to self-heal."

Ken Chye hid his surprise. "Sure, Mum. I'll call him now."

"Er, no need for this urgency, Kenny. You do it tomorrow when you meet in school, ok?"

"Sure, Mum." Ken Chye replied with a poker face. Inside, his heart soared to unprecedented levels. He had never felt more joyous or more relived in his life. Finally, his Mum had a change of mind. Never mind why. It was enough that his Mum wanted to self-heal. That alone was a miracle.

• • •

The appointment was fixed a few days later. On the day of appointment, the sun shone brightly. The sky was blue with patches of white clouds floating in it. Fresh breezes blew ever so often and the sound of birds' chirping filled the morning air. Never was there a finer day and Hai San rode to Sifu's house with a sense of joy and anticipation.

"It's good to see you again, Madam. I had half wondered if you had given up on healing yourself," Sifu Wang said smilingly as he welcomed his visitors to a sitting area in his back patio.

Madam Tang bit her lip and smiled uncertainly. "I'm not sure why I am here, Sifu, to be honest. But the boys seem to think that I need self-healing So, I've decided to give it a try." Her glance encompassed both Ken Chye and Hai San as she sat down.

Both boys glanced at each other and stifled a grin as they took their seats on either side of Madam Tang.

"I see," Sifu Wang replied conversationally. He cocked his head towards the kitchen door and said smilingly, "Oh, here's Maria with the refreshments."

When the coffee, freshly baked buns and appreciation were dispensed with, Sifu Wang leaned back in his chair and directed his gaze at Madam Tang and said, "As long as you keep an open mind and practice breathing, Madam, you will eventually be healed."

"Then I'll faithfully follow your instructions, Sifu, and I hope I can be fully healed as you say. But the minute things get worse, I'm going to stop," she declared.

Sifu Wang held up his hand and shook his head. "No, no, Madam, it is precisely when things get worse that you have to continue. That's a sign that things are rising to the surface for clearing. If you stop, you will do more harm than good. You have blockages that want to be cleared. *If* you ignore them, the symptoms will simply amplify themselves," Sifu Wang warned seriously. "How will you have peace then? Quite apart from the pain, do you want to be forever confronted with a lingering, nagging threat to your wellbeing?" he pointed out.

Madam Tang pouted, disliking what she was hearing.

"Let me explain it in another way, Madam. Perhaps then you will understand why breathing is so very important to healing," Sifu Wang offered.

"We are all Divine Consciousness, Madam. In other words, we are Gods. But the majority of us do not know this, you understand?"

Madam Tang gasped and then swallowed nervously. Her hand fluttered to her throat, visibly shaken.

Sifu Wang smiled in amusement. "I guess this is the first time you've heard this." He paused, took a few deep breaths and continued, "The story of ourselves is long. To cut the story short, somewhere, in the distant past, before we came to Earth, we made the decision to forget about who we are in order to play the Game of *Who Am I*."

"Sifu, why did we make this decision?" Ken Chye interrupted.

Sifu Wang smiled. "Good question. Can you answer, Hai San?" Sifu Wang looked at Han San.

Hai San felt all eyes on him. Heat began to creep up his neck. "Er," he began, brushing off a lock of hair. "It's because there was no understanding among the Gods in Heaven of their own powers and capability. In their ignorance, they had, somehow, caused the energy to be stuck in some part of the universe and this 'stuck' situation needed to be freed. Otherwise, the Universe would eventually come to a standstill through the mirror effect. So, the Gods in Heaven had to volunteer to come to Earth as part of an experiment to forget about who they are and to start from scratch to explore and learn in baby steps about who they are and how they could effectively work with energies to free the stuck situation." Hai San darted a look towards his teacher for confirmation.

"That's right," Sifu Wang confirmed. "And this is possible because the universe exists in holographs – by the way, do you know what a holograph is?" He looked at Madam Tang and then Ken Chye in turn.

Both mother and son shook their heads.

"Hai San, do you still remember what a holograph is?" Sifu Wang asked his pupil.

Hai San grinned. "It means that the whole is inside a part but at the same time, the part is also within the whole."

Sifu Wang smiled. "And so?" he prompted.

"And so it means that if we are within the universe, the entire universe is also within us," Hai San gushed out.

"Very good," his teacher commended. "So, when we breathe, really breathe, not the half-hearted surface breathing that most of us do every day, but the conscious full breath breathing, we activate the entire universe within us."

Madam Tang gasped again while Ken Chye whistled in surprise.

"But, that's not all, my dears," Sifu Wang said. "When we breathe deeply, we clear the blockages in our body just as we clear the blockages in the universe."

"Wow, now I know why Friend here is forever taking deep breaths," Ken Chye nudged Hai San in jest, Hai San let out a laugh and nudged back.

Sifu Wang looked on with amusement. "Breathing is also one of the ways of affirming our God Consciousness and bringing Magic back into our life," he revealed. "When we consciously breathe, we drive a message through our entire being that we are in charge, we are the King, the Emperor, the President of our Universe. If we do it often enough, the

Divinity within us starts to awaken and assume Its Role as the GOD IT IS. And lo and behold, every problem that we have will be resolved in its own way, including our Dis-eases. Now, do you understand why breathing is so important to us?"

Madam Tang weighed her words carefully. "If breathing is so important, why hasn't it been extolled as the Way to All Problems?"

"Good question," Sifu Wang acknowledged. "The Chinese, Indians and Indigenous Tribes of the World who practice the esoteric arts and sciences have known IT for centuries. But alas, the rest of the World has been *too* stuck on its own philosophy thus far to allow such a concept to break through. It takes a World in Crisis for people to question the existing beliefs and practices and seek alternative solutions."

He leaned back in his chair and breathed deeply of the fresh air in his garden. Madam Tang frowned as she carefully considered what Sifu Wang had just revealed. Both boys kept their heads bent and tried to be absorbed in their drinks while keeping their fingers crossed, lest Madam Tang decided to up and leave without the required coaching from Sifu Wang.

"Alright," she announced. "I'm already here, Sifu. I might as well take up your coaching even if it's as simple as Breathing."

Both boys heaved a silent sigh of relief. Sifu Wang looked at them both with amusement. Then he levelled a look at Madam Tang. "Very good, Madam," he said with a twinkle in his eyes.

"From now on, let breathing be something that you do consciously and unconsciously. Whenever you can remember, even if it is for a short moment while you are doing your house work or while you're driving, waiting at the traffic lights, talking to people, make an effort to take long deep breaths. As you do, you will be driving a message through your entire being that you are NOW Consciously Taking Charge. Can you do that?" Sifu Wang asked, raising his eyebrows.

"Yes, of course, Sifu. That's easy enough," Madam Tang replied.

"Good." Sifu nodded his approval.

"Could I do that, too, Sifu?" Ken Chye asked.

"Sure, Ken Chye. Deep Conscious Breathing is good for All," Sifu Wang replied. "It not only tells the Body who is in charge but it also clears the blockages, the stuck energies and the toxic wastes that have built up in the body."

"How long should I continue to do deep breathing, Sifu, before I see any result?" Madam Tang asked.

Sifu Wang thought for a second and replied, "It depends, Madam, on how major is the blockage. It can be a few days or a few weeks. However, you need to understand that once you start on this path, you cannot stop. There will continually be issues, aspects of Self rising up to the surface and you will continually have to release the old issues and integrate the aspects. It will, in time, become routine."

Madam Tang gasped in horror. "Do you mean I have to keep doing it for the rest of my life?"

"Surely you don't want to stop breathing?" Sifu Wang replied with a hint of amusement in his voice.

"What I mean is : do I have to consciously do it like I'm a patient for the rest of my life?"

Sifu Wang chuckled. "Of course not. That would be contrary to healing," he said. "You do it consciously like You're In Charge. Healing is an Attitude, Madam. If you imagine yourself as a patient, then you become a Patient. But if you imagine yourself as a Conscious Being who is taking charge of your life, then you should eventually be able to issue commands to your Self and your Body on how you want to Be."

"I see. Even if I'm just an ordinary person?" Madam Tang asked.

"Especially if you *feel* you are an ordinary person," Sifu Wang reaffirmed.

"Oh." Her eyes glistened but she smiled.

"Any more questions?" Sifu Wang asked.

Madam Tang shook her head. Both boys shook their heads, grinned and did a high five behind Madam Tang's back.

"In that case, we'll have a conscious breathing exercise for fifteen minutes," Sifu Wang said,

"Alright. Should we stand up or sit down?"

"It doesn't really matter, Madam. However you like it will be fine," Sifu Wang answered. "You can even lie down or walk around."

"I'll just sit then," Madam Tang decided.

"I'll walk around the garden," Hai San announced.

"Me, too," Ken Chye said, following Hai San out of the patio.

"Good," Sifu Wang said. "I'll see you all in fifteen minutes."

• • •

And so the routine for self healing was established. Every day Madam Tang and the boys (whenever they could remember) would do deep breathing for ten to fifteen minutes on their own while they would meet at Sifu Wang's place every Saturday morning for a mini breathing workshop. Madam Tang soon progressed to following the boys in walking around the garden barefooted to benefit from grounding.

Six weeks later, Madam Tang, looking fitter but thinner, rushed back from her Once-A-Month dinner with friends at the local restaurant, to search through her old handbag. Observing his mother's excited hurried movements, Ken Chye casually strolled up to his mother.

"Mum, you're back early," he said. "What are you looking for?" he asked curiously.

"Shh….shh…" She hushed up Ken Chye. She emptied out some old lipsticks, a bunch of old keys, various cards and bills and scraps of paper. Finally, she dug her fingers into the side pocket of the bag and took out a few sheets of receipts. She stared at each one of them in turn with wide open eyes and finally let out a squeal of delight.

Ken Chye grabbed the receipts to have a clearer look. "Is this a winning number, Mum?"

"Shh…,,yes!" she whispered and laughed gleefully. "We've won RM30,000.00 from Sports Toto," she revealed in a hushed tone, and hugged her son.

"Really, Mum?" Ken Chye whispered in an awed tone.

"Yes! Yes! We're going to take a break, have the roof repaired and order some new furniture," she whispered excitedly..

"Yippee!" Ken Chye exclaimed. "Where to, Mum? Could I have a new laptop also?"

"Cameron," Madam Tang replied to the first question. Then she pointed a finger at her son. "Only if you get an *A* for your Maths, Kenny. And I'm not joking."

"Aw, Mum, I've already tried my best," Ken Chye protested.

"You can do better, Kenny, if you don't spent so much time reading your comics or playing computer games," his mother admonished him.

Ken Chye put up his hands in surrender. "Ok, ok, I'll get an *A*."

Madam Tang grinned. "You make sure you do and the laptop is yours."

TWENTY-FOUR

THE STUDENT LEARNT TO RELEASE HIS VOWS OF POVERTY AND RESISTANCE TO WEALTH

"Hei, Friend, here's some fruity chocolates for you and tea for your Grandpa," Ken Chye called out and promptly dropped a plastic bag onto Hai San's carrier basket.

"Wow, thanks!" Hai San leaned over and peered into the bag. "You went to Cameron Highlands!" he exclaimed.

"Yup. It was a good break. See, I have a bit of tan now." Ken Chye showed Hai San his arms and legs. Hai San widened his eyes.

"What did you do there? Did you visit the morning market – the strawberry farm – the tea plantations –"

"Friend, we covered *all – all the places*," Ken Chye said smugly. "See this map –" Ken Chye drew out a map from his pocket. Hai San leaned forward to take a closer look. Ken Chye drew his finger across the paper. "We stayed here at Brinchang and we hiked to here and here and here and here and here."

Hai San looked at his friend enviously. "I've always wanted to visit Cameron Highlands," he said wistfully.

"You should go, Friend. It's really wonderful. You know, my mum cooked *herbal chicken soup* for dinner on the 1st night. Can you imagine or not, Friend? Taking steaming hot *herbal chicken soup with fragrant rice* at night when the air was so cold vapours practically poured out from our nose?" Ken Chye imitated a slurping sound followed by a blowing sound. Hai San's eyes rounded and he swallowed.

"And that's not all. We went to the Smokehouse Hotel in the morning and took English Breakfast. *Would you like poached eggs or scrambled eggs? How about baby mushrooms and cherry tomatoes?*" Ken Chye imitated. Hai San stared avidly at his friend before he swallowed hard again.

"See, we had to sit upright like the English people, tuck our napkin like this –" Ken Chye demonstrated to his friend "- and eat like this –" he made chewing movements with his mouth "without making any sound, otherwise other diners will stare at us," Ken Chye revealed gleefully.

Hai San widened his eyes. It all sounded so wonderful. And Ken Chye obviously enjoyed his stay there. If only he could visit Cameron Highlands, he thought to himself. Maybe he could convince his Grandpa to take a break. But his Grandpa had always said, '*Boy, it's the same everywhere. Don't spend unnecessarily.*'

He sighed. When it came to parting with money, his Grandpa had the tightest fist in the whole wide world.

"Why the sigh, Friend? A vacation in the Cameron is not that expensive." Ken Chye reasoned.

"Expensive or not, my Grandpa wouldn't spend the money. He had always said we should save and not spend unnecessarily," Hai San revealed sadly.

"Well, that's just too bad," Ken Chye sympathized. "A vacation can really make a lot of difference," he said. "My Mum came back with a bloom on her face and she is much happier now."

"That's good, Ken Chye!" Hai San said generously.

"Yeah, persuade your Grandpa and good luck to you, Friend!" Ken Chye waved a goodbye.

"Yeah, thanks," Hai San said. *Oh, God, how I wish! How I wish!* He inwardly prayed.

• • •

A fortnight later, Hai San was at Sifu Wang's place continuing with his lessons when he brought up the issue of the forthcoming lottery draw.

"Sifu, my school lottery will be drawn next month. Do you think I stand a chance to win?" he asked his teacher.

"Perhaps," Sifu Wang said smilingly. Hai San's heart gave a leap.

"Perhaps not." Hai San's heart sank and he stole a look at his teacher. *What does Sifu mean?*

"It depends on how steady your faith is in your Self, your God Self within, Hai San. What you have learnt and what you have experienced in the last few months is nothing short of phenomenal. What most people take to learn in decades, you did it in a matter of months. And that is really fantastic. However, being able to manifest at will, particularly for a lottery winning, is entirely a different matter. There are belief systems and aspects in all of us that work against our feelings of deservingness, particularly in getting fast money. That's why some people have to work hard all their life. As I have mentioned before, because of our past actions and our judgements of ourselves as having done wrong, we have really created beliefs of un-deservingness and therefore, these beliefs sit within our Personal Universe acting as the guard against any good that will come our way. To release these beliefs and the little selves that believe in our un-deservingness, we need to address the little selves and practise forgiveness regularly. Have you been doing that, Hai San?"

"Yes, Sifu," Hai San replied.

"Good. Keep doing it. It will clear a lot of guilt, anger and feelings of un-deservingness," Sifu Wang advised.

Sifu Wang leaned backed in his seat and contemplated for a few seconds. Then he smiled as if in acknowledgement. "There is also something else you need to clear very badly," he added gently.

Hai San sat up with a jolt, heart thumping wildly. "What's – what's that, Sifu?" he stammered.

"Vows, vows of poverty, Young Man. Somewhere in the past, you have made vows of poverty, and these are stopping you from getting the riches which you deserve," Sifu Wang stated.

"But – but, Sifu, why should I make any vows of poverty?" Hai San asked. "Isn't it stupid to do so?"

"Well, stupid or not, you had made it nonetheless. Perhaps," Sifu Wang said thoughtfully, "in the past, you were a monk or a priest, married to your religion, and you made a vow of poverty to serve God or mankind, not taking comfort or riches for your Self. Thus, this vow, being so serious as it was, remain with you until today. In a lot of people, it's not just ONE

VOW that prevails in the Personal Universe, Hai San. It's MULTIPLE VOWS. Vows which were made because of a series of tragic events that happened which the Self, in a fit of remorse, had mistakenly concluded happened as a result of the riches that one had enjoyed," Sifu Wang explained.

"Oh, Sifu, what kind of events would that be?" Hai San wailed out.

"Well, one could be born rich, without having a care in the world and as a result, one might have caused hardship or even death to another, due to one's recklessness or flaunting of one's wealth around. Say, if you had a fast carriage, in the latest style, and you flaunted it by driving recklessly around town and one day you just knocked down an old woman and killed her instantly, wouldn't you in a fit of remorse declare that you would never want to repeat that situation? "That situation" is what the Self might have interpreted as being wealthy and capable of hurting others. So because you connected the two things together, your Self vowed never to be wealthy again because to be wealthy is to have the capability to hurt others. That conclusion and interpretation are then saved within your Personal Universe. And there you are, in this lifetime, having a program of resisting wealth."

A moment of silence followed. Hai San looked down glumly at his feet. "Sifu, I was a Dominican nun before," he blurted out.

"Right, you probably took your vow of poverty then. And in one of your previous life you were also killed in your search for fortune. That might have crystallized your resistance to wealth."

Hai San looked beseechingly at his teacher. "Sifu, can you teach me to clear my programming?"

Sifu Wang smiled compassionately at his student. "Of course, Hai San. That's what you are here for." He leaned back in his seat and contemplated. "Suffice to say," he continued, "we should never form conclusions, interpretations or judgements. Whatever happens, happens. THINGS JUST ARE. THINGS JUST HAPPEN. Ok?"

Hai San nodded. *So, no conclusion, no interpretation and no judgement.*

"To clear your programming, you need to address aspects of your Self and say 'We now release all our fears, anger and guilt of being rich and comfortable. We now release our vows of poverty. We now release our vows of being poor and our resistance to wealth, comfort and luxury because they no longer serve us. We are ready now to proclaim our wealth that God intends for us. We are indeed rich beyond our wildest imagination. God intends for us to have surplus and to enjoy our life to the fullest capacity. We accept riches in abundance. Thank you, thank you, God, thank you, I am That I am, for abundance."

Sifu Wang quirked an eyebrow at the young man. "Can you do that, Hai San?"

"Yes, Sifu. Let me write it down so that I can remember."

"Sure, go ahead," Sifu Wang said.

Hai San quickly took out his notebook and scribbled down the contents of what he had just learnt.

• • •

That night Hai San took out his notebook and went through the practice of releasing his vows and fears. He breathed in a relaxed manner and thought of the Dominican nun. He gave his apology to her, "I am sorry. *Please* forgive me. *Please* forgive me for what you have gone through. *I love* you and God *loves* you. There was never any need to make a vow of poverty. THAT WAS A MISUNDERSTANDING! GOD really intends for you and us to be rich beyond our wildest dreams. What you went through is already over. Now we *release* our vows of poverty. We *release* our vows of poverty because they no longer serve us. We are on to something new now. Our current plan is to be rich without limits. Wealth is going to keep flowing into our life, our bank accounts, our pockets and we can see it in our lifestyle, our homes, our food, our transport, our clothes. WE THANK GOD, *I AM THAT I AM*, THAT WE ARE WEALTHY BEYOND MEASURE."

Hai San then thought of the young man that he was who left home to seek his fortune and met with his death. He gave his apology to the young man, "I *am* sorry. *Please* forgive me. *Please* forgive me for what you have gone through. I *love* you. I *love* you. We now *release* all our fears and resistance to being rich and comfortable. Whatever happened, *happened*. It's alright. It's not as a result of wanting to be rich. It's really ok to be rich. We now *release* our vows of poverty. We now *release* our resistance to being rich. God *intends* for us to be rich. God *intends* for us to have surplus. God intends for us to be comfortable in life. We shall be as what God intends for us. THEREFORE, WE *RELEASE* OUR VOWS OF POVERTY. HENCEFORTH, WE *ACCEPT* RICHES AND COMFORT. WE *ACCEPT* RICHES AND LUXURY. *I AM THAT I AM.*"

Hai San then brought the eunuch into his focus and he said, "I *am* sorry. *Please* forgive me. *Please* forgive me for what you have gone through. I *love* you. I *love* you. We now *release* all our fears and guilt for wanting wealth and position. Whatever happened, happened. It's not a result of wanting to be rich. It's just an experience we went through. God really likes us to be rich. God intends for us to have *surplus*. God intends for us to be *comfortable*. God intends for us to live a luxurious life. WE SHALL BE AS WHAT GOD INTENDS FOR US. WE *RELEASE* OUR VOW OF POVERTY. WE *RELEASE* OUR FEAR OF BEING RICH AND IMPORTANT. WE SHALL BE AS WHAT GOD INTENDS US TO BE. *THANK YOU* FOR ACCEPTING RICHES AND HIGH POSITION IN LIFE."

Hai San then went on to talk to the Red Indian chief, the lady spy, the corrupt ruler, the workaholic scientist and finally, the prostitute. He told the prostitute that he was, "I *am* sorry. *Please* forgive me. I *love* you. I *love* you for having gone through the experience and I *accept* you. I *accept* you as part of me. You are really an *angel*. GOD INTENDS FOR US TO EXPERIENCE EVERYTHING IN LIFE. SO *THANK YOU*. GOD INTENDS FOR US TO BE COMFORTABLE, HAPPY AND RICH. AND SO WE SHALL BE. *I AM THAT I AM.*"

He then walked around his room, breathing quietly in a relaxed manner. His whole body felt lighter, as if he had been relieved of a big load. The tension had left his joints, shoulders and neck. He could feel subtle energy humming within. And his heart chakra had opened. He went to bed with a big smile on his face.

TWENTY-FIVE

THE STUDENT LEARNT THE IMPORTANCE OF PRAISE AND GRATITUDE

The following Saturday, Hai San again met up with his teacher to continue with his lessons. They were walking barefoot in Sifu Wang's garden in companionable silence when Sifu Wang broached up the matter of releasing the vows of poverty. "So, Hai San, have you been releasing your vows of poverty?"

"Yes, Sifu. I've been doing that daily for the past week," Hai San replied.

"Good, good," Sifu Wang commended. "I want you to continue doing that for another week. Then you may stop and forget about the whole thing, ok?"

"Huh?" Hai San was nonplussed.

"You don't want to be doing that forever, do you?" Sifu Wang was amused.

"But, Sifu, what if I have saved many vows of poverty in my Personal Universe and I haven't yet released all of them by end of next week? Wouldn't the remaining unreleased vows interfere with my chances of winning the lottery?"

Sifu Wang smiled. "Then we shall cover all our bases, Young Man."

"How, Sifu?"

"You just put in a command, like this," Sifu Wang instructed. "I release all my vows of poverty and resistance to wealth and comfort made since time immemorial, for whatever reason, from the beginning of my earthly existence until now. I allow myself to be freed from declarations of any nature that impede my receipt of the flow of abundance of goodness and joy in my life. There are no right and wrong in life. I fully understand this fact. I am here to experience life. I shall therefore release all moral judgements of myself. I release all punishment of myself. I allow myself to experience free flow of abundance as God intends me to do. I allow myself to be safe and healthy. I allow myself to be rich, I allow myself to fully enjoy life. Can you do that?"

"Yes, Sifu.

"Can I get my pen and paper to write it down, Sifu?"

"Later. I'll give it to you again later. Now I want you to just do your grounding, relax and breathe deeply for the next ten to fifteen minutes."

"Ok, Sifu."

So, for the next ten to fifteen minutes, both teacher and student continued with their walk around the garden in a relaxed way while breathing deeply. The fresh breezes and early morning sun had given a lift to Hai San's spirits as had the breakfast he had shared with his teacher earlier. Wholewheat toast with a quarter inch thick slab of butter and half boiled eggs accompanied by local coffee ought to put any person in a good mood. He smiled happily as he breathed deeply of the scent of jasmine permeating the air in the garden.

When they had completed the grounding, Sifu Wang said, "Today I'm going to teach you one very important method that will enhance your power of manifesting whatever you want in life, Hai San. So, listen very carefully."

Hai San's heart missed a bit before it started to pound with excitement. He broke out in a grin. "Am I ready for it now, Sifu?"

Sifu Wang smiled with amusement. "Are you ready? Well, only you yourself will know. The test will be in the results. We shall take things a step at a time, though." He gestured to the garden seats a few meters away. "Take a seat."

Sifu Wang's eyes twinkled at Hai San's across the table. "Every one of us is a creator. Every one of us has the gift of manifestation. The only difference among us is whether we are manifesting consciously or unconsciously by default. Are we manifesting the things we want? Or are we manifesting what we don't want? That is the difference between mastery and no mastery, skillful or unskillful."

"The unskillful will go on, day in and day out, manifesting the same old things like a broken record. And why are they doing that, do you know, Hai San?"

"Er, ...they are unaware?" Hai San guessed.

"Yes, that's right. They are unaware of what they have programmed in their Personal Universe. They are unaware of the *Law of Mirrors*. They are unaware that what they have programmed in their Personal Universe will be reflected to them through the Law of Mirrors. So, day in, day out, they manifest what they have in their Personal Universe. And day in, day out, they complained about their lot in life, further saving what they don't like in their Personal Universe. And the Law of Mirrors keeps bringing it back to them. It's a vicious cycle, you see. They don't like it, they lament and complained about it and they keep getting it back."

"So, how can they break out of this vicious cycle, Sifu?" Hai San asked anxiously.

"They need to be conscious of what is happening, Hai San, and what they are doing to themselves. They need to stand up to the truth that they are responsible for everything that is happening to them. Until they do that, there is no rescue, really."

"Sifu, when they become conscious and they want to get out of the vicious cycle, how do they do it?"

"A strong intent for change is enough to change the energy structure in your Personal Universe to make way for new things to come in, Hai San. Look at your case as an example. You wanted to be a Super Being, right?"

"Yes, Sifu. I still want to be a Super Being."

"And you shall be, Young Man. Have no worries about that. When a person wants change, the whole universe will re-organise itself to allow that change to come about. Why is that, do you know, Hai San?"

Hai San scratched his head and frowned as he thought hard.

"Come on, it shouldn't be that difficult," Sifu Wang encouraged.

"Because we are Gods, Sifu?" Hai San ventured a guess.

"Bravo! I almost thought all my lessons to you have gone down the drain. Yes, because WE ARE GODS!" Sifu Wang declared triumphantly.

Hai San's heart glowed as he did an internal dance within himself.

"And look at you now, you have understood who you are, what you have undergone, what deficiencies and defaults you have accumulated from the past and are now clearing out progressively. The two last frontiers are your connection with God and acknowledging the presence of the God substance."

Connection with God? He, Hai San, was going to connect with God? Yippee! And he was also going to acknowledge the God substance? Double Yippee!!

"How do we connect with God, Sifu?" Hai San asked excitedly.

"There are various ways, Hai San, some of which I have taught you. Breathing consciously is one of them. Asking questions of yourself and getting answers through a pendulum is another way. Praying is also one way which most people do. Today, we are going to focus on a connection called *praising*. Do you know what praise is, Hai San?"

"Yes," Hai San said. "It's – like commending somebody with good words to show that we approve of them, isn't it?"

"Yes, excellent. *Praise* is an expression of admiration or approval using words that are positive and encouraging. So, today, we are going to praise who we are on the inside of us." Sifu Wang smiled at the expression of incredulity on his student's face.

"So, let's get started, mmm?"

Hai San nodded eagerly. "But, Sifu, why do we need to praise?"

"To get the attention of our inner selves, Hai San. For the majority of earth beings, the Divine Self is as yet un-awakened. Metaphorically speaking, the Divine Self is in deep slumber and cocooned so deeply within us that it would be difficult to get its attention unless we praise it. It only recognizes itself for what It Is as It has never been stepped down or split into duality. It is the unadulterated One. Only the Grandest Positive Attribute comes close to it." Sifu Wang explained.

"What kind of grand words can we use, Sifu?"

"Words such as *Almighty One, Most Glorious One, Most Magnificient One, Greatest Protector, Grandest Provider* and so on,' Sifu Wang replied.

"Super Duper!" Hai San exclaimed excitedly.

Sifu Wang chuckled. "Come, Hai San, give me a few other praise words that you would like to use to connect to God."

"Er – how about "Most Compassionate and Loving One?"

"Very Good. What else?"

"The Most Marvellous and Creative One? The Greatest ? ....The Greatest Genius...?" Hai San looked excitedly at Sifu Wang for guidance.

"Excellent, excellent! You've got the message well." Sifu Wang nodded approvingly.

"But, Sifu, how do we connect to God? Do we just speak out?" Hai San asked further.

"Yes, Hai San, you just speak out the attributes and then say whatever you want to say, like this : Dear God, dear *I am That I am*, the *Most Compassionate and Loving One*, the *Most Marvellous and Creative One*, the *Grandest Provider*, the *Greatest Genius*, The *One who is most Abundant in goodness*. You *are* the Orchestrator of the whole Universe. You make things happen *gloriously* and *joyfully* like no other. With your *Grace*, I ask for your Favour to shine upon my Project... etc etc, It's very simple. Now, do you get it?"

"Yes, Yes, Sifu!" Hai San nodded emphatically, eyes shining.

"Alright, Young Man, let's have a session of praise, shall we?" Sifu Wang suggested.

"Yes, yes, Sifu!" Hai San replied.

"Ok, let's get centred," Sifu Wang instructed.

Hai San sat up straight, half-closed his eyes and breathed deeply. His teacher observed him for a while before he led the praise session.

"Now, repeat after me, Hai San," Sifu Wang instructed. *"Dear God, Dear I Am That I Am."*

"Dear God, Dear *I Am* That I Am," Hai San repeated.

"*The Most Marvellously Creative One who is inside of Me as I am Inside of You*," Sifu Wang continued.

"*The Most Marvellously Creative One who is inside of Me as I am Inside of You.*"

"*You are The Greatest Genius.*"

"*You are The Greatest Genius.*"

"*The Most Wonderful Magician.*"

"*The Most Wonderful Magician.*"

"The Grandest Provider of Abundance and Joy."

"The Grandest Provider of Abundance and Joy."

"The Most Loving and Compassionate One, The All Forgiving One."

"The Most Loving and Compassionate One, The All Forgiving One."

"God, I Am That I Am – I love you and I thank you for the whole Universe."

"God, I Am That I Am – I love you and I thank you for the whole Universe."

"I thank you for Perfect Health."

"I thank you for Perfect Health."

"I thank you for my Wonderful House, I thank you for my wonderful family."

"I thank you for my Wonderful House, I thank you for my wonderful family."

"I thank you for my friends, I thank you for all the wonderful things that have come to me."

"I thank you for my friends, I thank you for all the wonderful things that have come to me."

"I love you, God, I love you, I Am That I Am."

"I love you, God, I love you, I Am That I Am."

"And I thank you so much for my life. You are the Orchestrator of the Whole Universe."

"And I thank you so much for my life. You are the Orchestrator of the Whole Universe."

"You enable my dreams and wishes to come true."

"You enable my dreams and wishes to come true."

"You bless me and the things that I do."

"You bless me and the things that I do."

"You give me my safety. You give me happiness."

"You give me my safety. You give me happiness."

"You give me good food. You give me luxury and comfort."

"You give me good food. You give me luxury and comfort."

"You give me freedom. You give me fulfilment, honour and respect."

"You give me freedom. You give me fulfilment, honour and respect."

"And I thank you, God, I thank you, I Am That I Am."

"And I thank you, God, I thank you, I Am That I Am."

"I love you. You are the Most Marvelously Creative One inside of Me as I Am Inside of You."

"I love you. You are the Most Marvelously Creative One inside of Me as I Am Inside of You."

"You are the Greatest Genius, My Grandest Provider and My Inmost Magician."

"You are the Greatest Genius, My Grandest Provider and My Inmost Magician."

"You Bless Me and All The Things That I Do. Thank you, God, Thank you, I Am That I Am."

"You Bless Me and All The Things That I Do. Thank you, God, Thank you, I Am That I Am."

"Alright, that's excellent," Sifu Wang commended.

"Alright, that's excellent."

Sifu Wang chuckled. Hai San jerked back and opened his eyes.

"Oops, sorry, Sifu," he said, smiling sheepishly at Sifu Wang.

Sifu Wang shook his head. "Not to worry, Hai San." He poured Hai San some green tea which Maria had brought and took a sip of his own.

"Did you notice that I added in *gratitude* into our praises just now?" Sifu Wang asked.

"Yes, Sifu. Why?"

"Because praise and gratitude come together. You cannot praise God and not feel grateful. One without the other is a bit imbalanced, you know. It's like yin yang. One is the Giver and the Other is the receiver," Sifu Wang explained. "From now on, I want you to praise your Godself at least twice a day everyday," he instructed. "Even if you are busy, you must make time for it."

"Yes, Sifu. What will happen when I do it?"

Sifu Wang smiled and his eyes crinkled merrily. "Magic will happen, of course."

Hai San's eyes gleamed in wonder. "*Magic! I love magic,*" he said happily.

TWENTY-SIX

THE STUDENT GRADUATED

Two weeks before the lottery draw, the school was abuzz with rumors of all kinds. Tim Gan had heard from the grapevine that Benjamin's father was going all out to determine his son's winning. He had hired a *fengshui* master to look over his house and had corrected certain deficiencies and that Benjamin, instead of using the back room of his house as the bedroom, had now shifted to the master bedroom. According to Benjamin's sister, their Mother had been grumbling non-stop about this move. The Number One Bookworm, Kong Ming, had decided that in this great race to win the lottery, he also should not be left out of the excitement. Apart from the Flying Star Fortune Tips, he had asked his Mother to buy pigeons from the market for him to free, eight pigeons to be precise and to be released on the eighth day of the month at eight o'clock in the morning. Another student had consulted his uncle who was an astrologer and the rumor was that he had been throwing copper coins into the river for seven consecutive days to ward off bad luck. A few senior students had sought their respective church groups to organize prayers while several in Hai San's class had sought their temple to do chanting and present offerings. Amidst all these excitement, Hai San was again derailed. Even though he had been faithfully doing his exercises, connecting with God, as instructed by Sifu Wang, he could not helped but be affected by all the shenanigans. So it was at 9.00am on Saturday, the last weekend before the lottery draw that he sought out Sifu Wang for some measure of assurance and confirmation.

But when Sifu Wang heard about all the activities that had been going on, he burst out laughing. In fact, he laughed so hard, that his whole body shook with mirth. Hai San was nonplussed. He could not understand how a situation as critical as this could be a laughing matter.

Finally, Sifu Wang sobered and settled down but retained his amusement. "Young Man, do not be worried. If you get it, you get it. If you do not, well, consider it as a *Great Experience*." Sifu Wang's eyes twinkled with humour.

"But, Sifu, why did you teach me all the secrets and then not be concerned about winning?" Hai San was perplexed.

"Because, Young Man, life is not about winning. It is about knowing *who* you are. It is about knowing that you *are* God also. It is about knowing that what God could do, you *too* could do. Until you internalize this fact and know, everything else is going to be achieved through struggle or by default. But when you know *who* you are and what you *could* do, the *whole universe* will move to accommodate your request. It's as simple as that."

Hai San was silent for a while as he absorbed this information. Then he said with a hint of vulnerability in his voice, "Sifu, I am not sure I really know who I am yet. Maybe I will one day. I know you have taught me a lot, Sifu. But it's still very new to me. And I am still very much influenced by external factors."

Sifu Wang looked at his student with great compassion. He took a step forward and hugged the young man. "You know more than you think or feel right now, Hai San. You just wait and see. Right now, it's understandable that you have doubts and you think other people with louder voices and even louder actions will command the show. But, I say, it is all *drama*. You have a higher chance of winning than all of them. Have *love* and *patience* for yourself, Hai San."

"I have a higher chance of winning than them?" Hai San was bemused.

"Certainly, Hai San. You are taught by a Master. Remember that. You do not know when things are going to turn in your favor. So, Never Give Up. The result is always dependent on how much faith and trust you have in yourself and in God."

"I'm going to teach you the ultimate secret to secure your dream," Sifu Wang continued in a matter of fact voice.

Hai San's eyes widened with surprise. *Sifu was going to teach him the ultimate secret?*

"But, first of all, you must clear your fears and worries, Hai San. Right Now. Do your deep breathing and grounding. Then, we'll get started," Sifu Wang instructed and left the Meditation Room.

Hai San promptly got up and walked around the Meditation room. It was a big room with hardly any furniture so walking and grounding was not a difficult matter. After about fifteen minutes, Sifu Wang came back.

"Alright now?" he asked his student,

"Yes, Sifu."

"Good. Now, the ultimate secret is nothing more than just acknowledging who we are and what our surrounding is. Got that?"

Hai San stilled. He didn't get it. He shook his head.

Sifu Wang chuckled. "Ok, who are we?" he asked his student.

"God. We are God."

"Excellent. We are God. Our consciousness is God. What is our surrounding?"

Hai San frowned. "God's creation?" he ventured.

"Excellent. Our surrounding is God's creation. Before it was manifested, what was it?" Sifu Wang asked.

"Er – was it a void?"

"Yes, that's right. It was a void, full of pure potential. Now, I want you to picture yourself as God consciousness at the centre of this void and just breathe. Breathe in a relaxed manner. If you like, speak out that creation is taking place."

"Shall I do it now, Sifu?"

"Yes, go ahead."

"How long should I take, Sifu?"

"A couple of minutes will do."

So, Hai San relaxed his limbs, sat cross-legged and closed his eyes. He imagined himself as the sole consciousness in the universe and the universe was a void. He breathed deeply in and out and acknowledged from his central position that creation was taking place in the void.

Then he opened his eyes and smiled at Sifu Wang.

"Ok, Hai San?"

"Yes, Sifu."

"Good, do that every morning for about a week. And don't worry about anything else. Just focus on the fact that you *are* God also and that your surrounding is a void, full of pure potential and creation is happening."

"Thank you, Sifu. I feel much better already!" Hai San smiled happily.

• • •

The lottery draw was held in the school hall at 3.30pm on a Sunday. Despite all the excitement of fellow students and their family members and friends, Hai San was not available to join in the festivity as he had to be on duty in directing traffic to the makeshift car park beside the school ground. Almost one thousand visitors turned up to witness the lottery draw and by 3.00pm, the makeshift car park at the side of the school ground was nearly full and Hai San and his friends on duty had to improvise and allow for back to back parking in order to maximize on the space.

As students on duty, both Hai San and Ken Chye were not permitted to leave their post until the last of the visitors had left the car park. So it was not a surprise that they do not know the lottery draw results until 4.50pm when an excited Tim Gan rushed into the car park, red faced from his three flights marathon down the school stairs and across the school driveway to the makeshift car park, to share the breaking news.

"Hai San! Hai San!" Tim Gan shouted from afar. "It's your ticket, isn't it?" He vigorously waived a piece of paper in the air.

Hai San's heart skipped a bit and then pounded madly as adrenalin began to surge. Sweat poured from his temple as he rushed to meet his friend. "Let me see!" he shouted excitedly.

However, before Hai San could reach Tim Gan, Ken Chye had already snatched the piece of paper from Tim Gan and waved it in the air. "Hohoho, it's my ticket, it's my number!" he teased.

"Stop it, Ken Chye! Let me see the number!" Hai San tried to grab at the paper. But Ken Chye was a good dodger. He waived the paper this way and that way and did an imitation of a warrior dance to prevent the other two from getting the paper. Finally, Hai San did the unthinkable. He tickled Ken Chye on his ribs.

"Ah –ha-ha, ah-ha-ha," Ken Chye protested and dropped the paper on the ground which was promptly picked up by Hai San while Tim Gan stumbled.

Hai San stared at the 2nd placing which was an unknown number to him. He frowned and directed a look at Tim Gan. "Friend," his voice rang out, full of disappointment. "It's not my number!"

Tim Gan looked at him weirdly. "You've got two numbers drawn, Hai San. I know because we both bought our tickets in sequence."

Hai San stared at his friend dumbly before looking back at the paper again. Heart racing, his eyes scrolled down each placing for his numbers. His eyes reached down to the bottom on the list and backtracked again to the top. And then – there it was! His heart skipped a bit and pounded more vigorously now – the winning number – the first prize which was a BMW sports series, but the ticket was now owned by Sifu Wang. He couldn't help a twinge of regret. He breathed deeply and his eyes darted through the other numbers again and spotted another number with almost the same reading as the first winning number except for the last digit. To his shock, the prize was a vacation for two in Cameron Highlands. He didn't even know that there was a prize for a vacation in Cameron Highlands!

He dropped down onto the pavement, shocked. It was all too much for him to take in.

"*Hei, Friend. You lucky devil,* how did you manage to get two numbers drawn?" Ken Chye dropped down beside Hai San and peered into the piece of paper Hai San was holding. "*Geez,* where *are* your numbers? *Which prize? Where?*"

Tim Gan sat on the other side of Hai San and leaned sideway, nudging his shoulders. "*Lucky devil! Lucky devil* is the right word! How *did* you manage it?"

Hai San breathed deeply a few times, trying to grapple with the way things have turned out. And all of a sudden, it was as if a light had been shone onto him. He began to smile in wonder. Sifu is really a Master, he thought. And he himself – well – he had just graduated, hadn't he – with visible proof?

"The 1st prize belongs to Sifu Wang. He bought the ticket from me actually." Hai San revealed. "My own winning ticket is the one drawn for a vacation in Cameron Highlands."

Ken Chye whistled. "Not coincidence, is it? You had wanted to go to Cameron very much."

Hai San grinned. "I didn't know that there was ever this kind of prize."

"There wasn't," Tim Gan revealed. "The original prize was for a vacation in PulauRedang. But the sponsors changed it to Cameron Highlands at the last minute. And they topped it up with a pocket allowance of RM1,000.00."

"Wow, our friend is very rich now!" Ken Chye teased Hai San.

Red faced, Hai San laughed it off. "Well, I'm very happy that I won something that I had wished for. What about you both?"

Ken Chye smiled and shrugged. "No such luck, Friend. You already took our share!"

"Hei, that's not fair!" Hai San protested laughingly.

Tim Gan smiled sheepishly. "Maybe next time."

"Yeah, next time," Hai San said. "What happened to Benjamin? And Muthu who threw the copper coins?"

"Well, Benjamin's sister said their Mother was demanding for her master bedroom back! And Muthu said he was swearing off gambling altogether."

Ken Chye asked, "What about our Number One Book Worm?"

Tim Gan replied, "Nothing. Just a lot of noise."

He looked at both of his friends in turn and they all laughed headily for a while.

"But somebody from the Fifth Form bagged the Perodua," Tim Gan added. "And do you know – his father holds a car dealership from Perodua. Isn't that a coincidence?"

"No coincidence!" Hai San declared. "It's the *Law of Mirrors*. He probably eats, sleeps and breathes perodua everyday. That's why."

"What?" Both Ken Chye and Tim Gan looked at each other in puzzlement.

• • •

Hai San rushed home as soon as he could. First he told his grandfather about the prized vacation and both old man and young man cheered on their good fortune. Then Hai San telephoned Sifu Wang and told him about the good news. Sifu Wang happily accepted the news without showing any sign of surprise. He then told Hai San that a celebration was called for and promptly invited them to lunch the following Saturday at his home.

• • •

They were all seated in Sifu Wang's dining room where an array of delicious seafood, meat and vegetables were being served by Maria. Lily sat at her grandfather's right, intermittently peeping at Hai San while Hai San sat at Sifu Wang's left and Hai San's grandfather sat opposite Sifu Wang.

Sifu Wang raised his glass for a toast. "Cheers to you, Brother, may you live a long, happy and healthy life."

"Cheers, Brother, I salute you for your wisdom and thank you for taking my grandson under your wing. Congratulations to you, too, for winning the 1st prize."

"Thank you, Brother. It has been a pleasure!" Sifu Wang replied.

Hai San raised his glass to Sifu Wang, "Cheers, Sifu! Thank you for your coaching. Without it, I wouldn't have been able to win a holiday vacation to Cameron Highlands."

Sifu Wang raised his glass to Hai San. "Cheers, Hai San. Thank you for selling me your lottery ticket. Allow me to congratulate you as well as you have a 20% share of the winning as referral fee."

Hai san was nonplussed. *20% share of the winning! Oh, what does that mean?*

Sifu Wang smiled at his confusion. "Hai San, a referral fee is like a mini commission. I am arranging for you to have that because you forego your ticket to sell to me. I will not be using the car myself, though. Lily's Mother will have the privilege but I'll ask her to pay you the 20%. You deserve it. This 20% can buy you a Perodua in a few years' time when you are ready to drive it."

Hai San's mouth gaped open. His heart warmed over and he was dumbstruck by Sifu's generosity.

His grandfather touched his shoulder. "Thank Sifu, Boy. Where are your manners?"

Suddenly, Hai San sprang to life. "Thank you, Sifu, thank you so much."

Sifu Wang nodded smilingly in acknowledgement. "Well done, Young Man. You got your Perodua finally."

"And my trip to Cameron Highlands with my Grandpa, too!" Hai San added happily.

"Ah Gong, I also want to *cheers*," Lily whispered.

"Oh, poppet, you wish to make a toast? Ok…ok…what do you want to drink to?" Sifu Wang asked. He filled up the older man's glass with red wine and added fruit cordial to Hai San's and Lily's glasses.

"I want to drink to my baby brothers' good health. I hope they don't cry too much!" the little girl said.

Sifu Wang laughed and gave her a kiss on the forehead. "So *cheers* to good health for the newly born babies!"

"*Cheers to good health for the newly born babies! Cheers! Cheers!*" they all chorused.

**** The end ****

www.ingramcontent.com/pod-product-compliance
Lightning Source LLC
Chambersburg PA
CBHW030324080526
44584CB00012B/692